Margaret Scott was born in the English city of Bristol in 1934.

After reading English at Cambridge she worked in a false eye-lash factory, taught in two schools and in 1959 emigrated to Tasmania with her first husband and their sixteen-month-old son. Although she arrived determined to return to Britain after two years, she is now addicted to Tasmania and would not live anywhere else. For twenty-four years she taught in the English Department of the University of Tasmania, retiring in 1989 to become a full-time writer.

Margaret has written three books of poetry: *Tricks of Memory*, *Visited* and *The Black Swans*, a novel, *The Baby Farmer*, and, with Vivian Smith, edited *Effects of Light: The Poetry of Tasmania*. She has also written numerous articles, poems and short stories for periodicals in Australia, New Zealand, UK and the US, and a television script for Artist Services. She is a well-known public speaker and has appeared in 'World Series' debates on television.

PORT ARTHUR

A Story
of
Strength
and
Courage

Margaret Scott

RANDOM HOUSE
AUSTRALIA

Random House Australia Pty Ltd
20 Alfred Street, Milsons Point, NSW 2061
http://www.randomhouse.com.au

Sydney   New York   Toronto
London   Auckland   Johannesburg
and agencies throughout the world

First published in 1997
Copyright © Margaret Scott 1997

National Library of Australia
Cataloguing-in-Publication data:

Scott, Margaret, 1934–.
    Port Arthur: a story of strength and courage.
    ISBN 0 09 183521 6.
    1. Mass murder – Tasmania – Port Arthur. I. Title.
364.1523099464

Cover photograph by Geoffrey Lea
Designed and typeset by text-art
Printed and bound by Griffin Press

To past and present victims of violence

~

*Yea, though I walk through the valley of the shadow
of death, I will fear no evil: for thou art with me; thy
rod and thy staff they comfort me.*

— PSALM 23:4

Acknowledgements

I would like to thank all those who have contributed to this book by allowing me to interview them or quote from written material; other residents of Tasman and members of the Tasman Trust for their support; my family for their forbearance; Patricia Parker for her work in preparing the manuscript; and the many others who helped me in various ways including Maggie Best, Mary Blackwood, Ruth Blair, John Edwards, Maree Heron, James Parker, Peter Pierce, Walter Pridmore, Tom Purdon, Margo and Michael Roe, Margaret Sullivan, Lyn Tranter and staff of the Morris Miller Library at the University of Tasmania.

CONTENTS

~

THE TASMAN PENINSULA

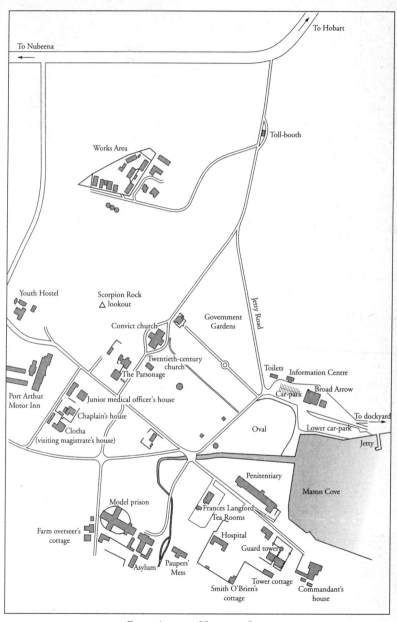

PORT ARTHUR HISTORIC SITE

INTRODUCTION

~

On the day of the memorial service in St David's Cathedral in the centre of Hobart, you could hear the traffic lights clicking in the silence of the city streets.

In about 1978, a friend offered to lend us a holiday shack on the Tasman Peninsula. All the rest of the family were busy doing other things, so I came down for a week with Sarah, the youngest, who was six. We had a wonderful time, and immediately the place began to cast its spell over us. We drove along bush tracks to explore places like Lime Bay and Fortescue Bay, where Sarah learned to swim in the lagoon. It seemed— it is—wonderfully beautiful, and after a time, this beauty moved me very much because it had endured through so much: the destruction of a group of Aborigines from the Oyster Bay tribe, whose middens are scattered behind many of the beaches; the use of the place as a prison of the grimmest kind; and years of logging which took out almost all the tall timber—not to mention whaling, trawling, mining and so on, all done with no thought of preserving anything or putting anything back. And yet, from our little boat in the middle of a bay, the white stems of the gum trees, the aquamarine of the shallows, the far hills, looked pristine, as though it was the morning of the world. The place had a power to restore itself and while I felt some relics should be preserved it was wonderful to see the way the bush was swallowing the convict coal-mines and growing over the graves.

We began to come here as often as we could. Sometimes my partner Michael Scott came, and one or more of the older children. I started reading about the Peninsula and meeting some of the people who lived here. I read their stories in the History Society's first *Chronicles* and saw that many families, like the land itself, had come through bad times, endured and gone on to lead sensible, generous lives.

When Michael died in 1984, I made three decisions about the future: first, that I should find a project that would keep me from brooding, something that would absorb any spare time and energy that I might have; second, that I should eventually take early retirement from my job to become what I had always hoped to be—a full-time writer; third, that I should one day sell my house in Hobart and move to the Tasman Peninsula.

Looking at those three aims, I saw that what I had to do was to scour the Peninsula, not for some ready-made Shangri-la, but for a house which could be gradually moulded into the ideal writer's retreat. With the help of a friend, I found 'Tara' which had once been a very beautiful Federation house and the hub of a busy fruit-growing property. By 1985, it was home only to possums, rats and swallows, and was about to be turned into a quail shed. Restoring 'Tara' took years but it was a wonderfully satisfying exercise which helped me through a difficult time. I finally moved in as a permanent resident in 1991.

Although I have written two novels and various scripts, stories and articles, I am primarily a poet. Since discovering the Peninsula, I have written many poems about it and about the house in which I live. Often these poems are concerned in some way with renewal, restoration or reconciliation. I felt very hesitant about writing *Port Arthur: A Story of Strength and Courage* because I was one of the lucky ones. I didn't lose any of my family on 28 April. I wasn't wounded. I was safe at home on that day and, when people started to ring up at about three in the afternoon asking about the shooting at Port Arthur, insisted that the shooting could not be real. I explained soothingly that the State Emergency Service often conducted training exercises on the Peninsula and must be engaged in some simulated incident involving gunfire. It was at least four o'clock before I turned on the radio and heard the atrocious truth which had long ago been flashed across the world.

~

On the morning of 29 April the Port Arthur massacre was front-page news across the world. Millions of people who thought Tasmania was somewhere in Africa—if they had heard of it at all—pored over maps in which a little, shield-shaped island was shown hanging beneath the bulk of mainland Australia like a drip under a jelly bag. It looked as though the quintessence of the huge continent was draining down into the smallest of the Australian states. Fanciful as this impression might have seemed, there was more truth in it than most readers in London or New York would have imagined.

For decades, movements and events which have seemed diffuse or partial in Australia at large have become, in Tasmania, concentrated and extreme. The island is a place of weird contrasts and fierce polarities. In its clear light, issues take on a harder edge and battle lines stand out more sharply. Usually it is the ultra-conservatives who are seen on the mainland as typifying their state, but the place has always been home to some of the most vigorous radicals in the country. The list runs over the decades from visionary reformers like the penologist, Alexander Maconochie, to gay activists like Rodney Croome, or the group who founded the world's first environmental political party in the early 1970s.

In Tasmania the best and the worst trends in Australian life reach some kind of climax or, at least, can be seen for what they really are. The arrival of the white invaders brought suffering and death to indigenous people in every corner of the mainland. In Tasmania not one full-blooded Aborigine survived the impact of the invasion. Yet at other times the people of the island state have typified Australia at its best.

In 1967 when the south of the state was devastated by one of the worst bushfires in the nation's history, Tasmanians forgot their differences and met the catastrophe with courage and generosity. The victims were helped by a torrent of aid from beyond their own state, and natural disasters on the Australian mainland have evoked similar responses. Perhaps the Tasmanian reaction shone out with special clarity because in a small, remote community, nobody escapes the pain, and a population of less than half a million can react—or be seen to react—as one.

Since mid-1987, Australia has witnessed a series of multiple killings: Melbourne's Hoddle and Queen Streets; Sydney's Canley Vale, Surry Hills and Strathfield; the murderous spree of Leonard Leabeater and his accomplices which ended with a siege in northern New South Wales. On 28 April 1996 a Tasmanian gunman, armed like the Strathfield killer with a semi-automatic weapon, embarked on the same kind of indiscriminate slaughter. Like Leabeater he went to ground, apparently with hostages, in an isolated property that was quickly surrounded by police. Only the death toll in the Port Arthur massacre was up to seven times higher than in any one of the six mainland shootings.

The effects of Martin Bryant's rampage were felt across the world. Two of the thirty-five victims who lost their lives came from Kuala Lumpur. Two of the wounded were Canadians. Others, like Robert Salzmann and his wife, Helene, who were shot in a car at the Port Arthur toll-booth, had relatives and friends in other countries. Nobody knows exactly how many people from overseas visited Port Arthur on that fatal Sunday. Nobody knows how much psychological damage they sustained or what nightmares they carried home.

Many of those who died were from mainland Australia: twelve from Victoria, six from New South Wales, two from South Australia, one from Western Australia. Others from Winston Hills or Merryland, from Vermont in Victoria or Warradale in South Australia were amongst the injured. Still other mainland visitors who witnessed part of the slaughter or escaped by the skin of their teeth are certain that their lives have been changed for ever. The whole nation mourned.

In Tasmania, which lost twelve of its residents, the list of dead and injured was, perhaps, shorter than might have been expected, given that the shooting had occurred on Tasmanian soil.

But in Tasmania, where so many people, from paramedics to pilots, had been drawn into the vortex created by the shooting, where everyone knew somebody involved, the disaster became inescapable. On the day of the memorial service in St David's Cathedral in the centre of Hobart, you could hear the traffic lights clicking in the silence of the city streets.

If the island state represents a kind of distillation of elements in mainland life, then the Tasman Peninsula, which lies about eighty kilometres south-east of Hobart, is Tasmania's Tasmania. It is breathtakingly beautiful and astonishingly varied, combining rainforest with heath or scrub and green farmlands with rocky headlands. From Eaglehawk Neck, the isthmus running between the Tasman and Forestier Peninsulas, you can look west to Norfolk Bay with its quiet waters, tree-fringed shores, egrets, oyster catchers and black swans, or east to the great breakers of Pirates' Bay, rolling in past towering cliffs and the fantastic Gothic shapes of The Lanterns and Tasman's Arch.

This was Lieutenant-Governor Arthur's natural penitentiary where a chain of convict probation stations grew up around the fringe of Norfolk Bay and a gaol for second offenders was built near the head of the southern inlet, known, like the prison itself, as Port Arthur. So while the convicts transported to Van Diemen's Land were worked as assigned servants or in government gangs all over the accessible parts of the colony, the Tasman Peninsula became, in effect, the gaol of a gaol.

When the prison at Port Arthur was closed in 1877 and land on the Peninsula was opened to settlers, some of the first to arrive were the descendants of former convicts.

The six Greatbatch brothers, who set up a farm at Nubeena in the early 1880s, were the sons of a man who had served time at Port Arthur. Other descendants of Port Arthur inmates, like the Palmers and the Gathercoles, settled still closer to the abandoned gaol. You might have thought that they would have turned on the penitentiary, the Commandant's house and the Model Prison and torn them stone from stone. But that is not what happened.

It is true that the Historic Site today is much less crowded with buildings than the model of the convict township set up in the Site's museum. Any remaining structure made of wood was swept away in the bushfires that devastated Port Arthur in the 1890s. But afterwards, instead of carrying on where the fires had left off, the people who had come to live in the area set about adapting the remains of the prison to their own purposes.

The Commandant's house and the Junior Medical Officer's residence became hotels. Shops and new houses sprang up. The Parsonage, damaged in the fires, was restored to serve as the post office, in what was fast becoming a bustling town-ship, known now as Carnarvon. Most significantly, the citizens of Carnarvon carefully restored the Asylum, which had housed those driven mad by the silence of the Model Prison, and used it as a social centre. Here, under one roof, were the local school, one of the best dance floors in the state, and, ultimately, the Tasman Council Chambers. While all across Australia and espe-cially in the former Van Diemen's Land a new generation was seeking ways of living with or living down 'the hated stain', the people of the Tasman Peninsula set up an extraordinary metaphor. They preserved the past to become the ground for social interaction and the management of their own destiny. They made the suffering and madness of an earlier time the site of their children's education and planted in it their hopes for the future.

Since the days when this was done, the complexion of the Tasman community has undergone some changes. The place, like the rest of the state and much of mainland Australia, gradually built up prosperous primary industries which, in the 1960s began to feel the chilling winds of change. The bottom fell out of the fruit-growing industry when the United Kingdom joined the European Economic Community, and the march of agri-business with its tenet, 'Get Big or Get Out' has put an end to the dairy herds. Now it is bearing down on the smaller chicken farms. Tourism is the community's hope for the future with the Port Arthur Historic Site as the Peninsula's major employer and the magnet that draws tourists to the restaurants, hotels and shops scattered along the Arthur Highway, to the Bush Mill and the Taranna Devil Park. Unemployment is at least 18 per cent and the young tend to drift away to the city. But, at the same time, as farms or tracts of bushland belonging to farmers have been offered for sale, new residents have arrived.

The population of the whole Tasman Municipality, which includes the Forestier Peninsula to the north, is still less than 2500, although during holiday periods when shack-owners and campers arrive and all the tourist accommodation is full, the number soars to close on nine thousand.

The permanent residents are a mixed group so that, true to form, Tasman represents something very like a cross-section of Tasmanian—or even Australian—society at large, although its dyed-in-the-wool conservatives and its alternative lifestylers are, perhaps, more highly coloured than in most places. There are families who have been on the land for six generations alongside retirees from Sydney, new-age devotees from Europe, writers, artists, craftspeople, fishermen, back-hoe operators and builders, Jehovah's Witnesses, Anglicans, a Zen Buddhist who knew Kerouac in the 1960s, a nursing sister who is passionate about Celtic iconography and makes exquisite quilts and a Chinese businesswoman who has joined the CWA.

The events of 28 April fell upon this community like a cyclone. Seven of its members, including two small children, one of the two teenagers who were shot and two of the younger adults, died at Port Arthur. Brigid Cook, the chef at the Broad Arrow restaurant, was physically wounded. A very large proportion of the community were closely involved in some way: as people bereaved of close friends or family members; as employees at the Historic Site who were present when the killing started and afterwards did all they could to help; as witnesses to the shooting that took place between the Site and Seascape, where the gunman took refuge; as helpers, like the church-goers who arrived by chance and began directing traffic to safety, or others, like the doctors, ambulance drivers and members of the local branch of the State Emergency Service, who were called to the massacre scene. None of these people will ever forget that sunny autumn Sunday afternoon.

... any recovery needs to be community driven.

Everyone on the Peninsula knew at least one of the dead; many knew them all. Nobody could insulate themselves from the general grief. And in the week that followed the massacre, people began to realise that the community was facing other forms of loss as well. The tourist buses stopped running. Once the journalists who had flooded in from all over the world had gone away, the hotels, restaurants and holiday units were left empty.

But the people of Tasman are fighting back, as they have fought back before. They have no monopoly on pain, of course, or on courage. Yet, as has happened in the past, this small community in Australia's deep south has become a crucible in which evil and death and the struggle to overcome these forces stand out in their starkest colours so that all of us can see more clearly who we are and what we might become.

I have put together this version of Port Arthur's history, including the events of 28 April 1996, and what happened in the Tasman region after the day partly because I want to acknowledge the courage and dedication shown by so many. In particular I want to show that, while the help received by the people of the Peninsula has been wonderfully generous, they have done more to advance their own recovery since the massacre than is generally realised.

Some who have worked immensely hard to bring the community through its trauma believe there are lessons to be learned from their experience. This book, I hope, will allow voices like that of Elaine Ball, one of Tasman's two community health sisters, to be more widely heard. After ten months of trying to alleviate the effects of the massacre she believes that each person must be allowed to recover at his or her own pace. According to Elaine, any recovery needs to be community-driven: although all attempts to overcome disaster share common features, the recovery path after each event is unique and cannot be predicted in any detail. Care must also be taken of the carers so that they are not left without support or allowed to burn themselves out.

Beyond these issues are other broader questions which relate to both the violence enacted at Port Arthur in its time as a prison and the horrors of the recent massacre. In February 1997, when this book was almost finished, a number of controversies erupted over the preservation and future development of the Port Arthur Historic Site. These were, in essence, debates about how we see the past and why it matters to us. Ostensibly the arguments were concerned with convict buildings and the presentation of violent lives from over a hundred years ago, but they were—and are—intimately linked with how we see the events of 28 April 1996, and what they too mean for us all now.

This book is in part an attempt to canvass some common attitudes to the inhumanities of the past. The most obvious of these is the kind of denial which evinces itself in demands that Port Arthur should be razed to the ground, 28 April totally forgotten and Martin Bryant never mentioned or thought of again. Seemingly opposed to this willed amnesia is the sensationalism which colours up the horrors of the flogging yard and the blood-stained café, the cannibal convict and the pale-eyed Monster of New Town until places and people become so hideous and grotesque that they cease to have any relevance to real life. In the end both attitudes have the effect of distancing the observer from the past and evading the hard questions raised by a legacy of violence. Both are fundamentally different from the steady effort to go on trying to see things with honesty and compassion, an effort without which there can never be any genuine recovery on the Tasman Peninsula or anywhere else.

The account I have given of 28 April is based primarily on the transcript of Martin Bryant's sentencing hearing held in the

Supreme Court of Tasmania on 19, 20 and 22 November 1996. The step-by-step description of events set out by the Director of Public Prosecutions, Damian Bugg QC, and Crown Counsel, Nicholas Perks, was based in turn on the findings of a Police Task Force led by Superintendent Jack Johnson and consisting of twenty-two full-time investigators assisted by teams of forensic scientists and other experts. Material from the transcript is supplemented by a range of eye-witness reports, some drawn from newspapers and some from interviews with a random collection of people who were present at Port Arthur on the afternoon of 28 April and were later kind enough to allow me to record their impressions. Since I was anxious to avoid distressing anyone who was reluctant to recall their experience or who might be further damaged by doing this, my witnesses are either people who responded to an advertisement that I placed in the local *Gazette* or people whom I had already met as neighbours or fellow members of some committee, people who would, I felt, not be upset by being asked to contribute to the book and knew me well enough to say 'no' if they wanted to. This haphazard method of selection has produced a very mixed bag of witnesses. Some were at the centre of things, some were not. Certainly there are points at which, even within this small group, perceptions of the same scene or event vary dramatically from one account to another. One witness who arrived at the Site shortly after 2.00 p.m. saw the situation as already well under control while another, arriving later, saw it as wildly chaotic. Such variations are themselves part of what occurred and, at the same time, serve as a reminder that the broader account, of which they are part, is itself inevitably limited and skewed. Of the hundreds of people who were at the

Site on that day, I have mentioned only a handful. And I have no doubt that the acts of bravery, self-sacrifice and compassion that I have mentioned also represent only a fraction of all those that were performed.

No-one can pay tribute to everybody who was, or is, involved. The police took statements from over six-hundred people who were at the scene of the massacre, or directly affected in some way. Afterwards, thousand of others gave help of all kinds. Offers of assistance came from all over the world. On the Peninsula everyone I know did something to help somebody and to pull the community through. Again I can reveal only a tiny fraction of all this.

I have invited other Peninsula residents to give their views of the Tasman Peninsula and the people who live there. Together they represent a kind of cross-section of Peninsula society, or at least give some idea of its diversity and of the different ways in which the massacre touched the lives of everyone living in the area, even when they were not actually shot at themselves and suffered no close personal loss.

While writing this book I have discovered that what people endured, and are still enduring, is even more dreadful than I had imagined; the struggle to recover much more protracted and intense than I had thought, so that the renewal, which is coming, appears to be even more of an achievement than I had believed it to be.

THE SITE

~

A lot of violence has happened there. It must be the most violent place in Australia. It seemed the right place.

— MARTIN BRYANT

In December 1855 a proclamation was approved, substituting the name 'Tasmania' for that of 'Van Diemen's Land'. This was a relief to colonists of the better sort who knew all too well that, as 'Van Diemen's Land', their home had become notorious throughout the British Empire. Now, after more than a century of quiet in which much of the world beyond the ambit of Tasmanian tourist promotion has forgotten both the old name and the new, the island has become notorious again. And, of course, not just any part of the island. The tragedy of 28 April 1996 was played out at Port Arthur, the most widely known of Van Diemen's Land's penal settlements, the darkest stain on its feared and tarnished name.

Once the colony had been renamed, the attempt to purge the place of its past led on to other changes. On the Tasman Peninsula, the former probation stations of Wedge Bay, Cascades and Impression Bay became, in time, the free settlements of Nubeena, Koonya and Premaydena. But at Port Arthur, which was supposed to become known as Carnarvon, the power of the old name proved too strong. Once a byword for the darkest facets of life in the nineteenth century, it has acquired an even more sinister reputation in the last decade of the twentieth.

So far as I know, nothing quite like this has occurred before. None of the Australian mass murders of the past took place at sites with a well-attested history of exceptional violence, pain and misery. Neither San Ysidro, California, where James Huberty killed twenty-one victims in July 1984, nor the English town of Hungerford where Michael Ryan shot dead sixteen people in August 1987 are places where people gathered to contemplate a peculiarly dark passage in their nation's history.

On 28 April 1996 at Port Arthur, the reality of an earlier spate of suffering and death flashed for a moment, as though lit by a bolt of lightning. Many of those who heard gunshots thought a re-enactment of past events was in progress.

One witness inside the Broad Arrow Cafe imagined the people falling and dying around him were playing out some drama involving convicts and musketry. Only when he saw a woman shot in the temple and blood spurt from her head did he realise that he was watching a murderer in action then and there.

It was as though the ghost of the convict past, which seemed to have been confronted and made tame, had come back, unplacated, to demand that we take stock all over again.

Others experienced a less terrible sense of double vision but became aware of the shadow of earlier cruelties moving behind the horrors of that April Sunday. It was as though the ghost of the convict past, which seemed to have been confronted and made tame, had come back, unplacated, to demand that we take stock all over again.

One reaction to this was to turn quickly away, to persist in the familiar denial of the past which, in the days before convict ancestors became fashionable, led to the wholesale destruction of records, the ostracism of aged relatives and the re-jigging of family histories. In the week following the massacre there was a lot of talk of Tasmania's 'loss of innocence' as though the 'holiday isle' of the tourist brochures had never been Van Diemen's Land at all. At this members of the Aboriginal community protested—as well they might—that the history of the island state was very far from innocent since it encompassed the destruction of their forebears. There had been other massacres, other women and children—members of the indigenous population—shot down by men with guns. And some commentators, at least, recognised that innocence had not been the most prominent characteristic of mid-nineteenth century Port Arthur. The journalist Lindsay Simpson, amongst others, engaged in some trenchant criticism of the way in which the convict past, even when not denied, is habitually sanitised and sweetened. She went on to insist that the horrific events of this past as well as those of the present should be treated with a veracity which 'shows respect for those who died'.

Finally, there were those who laid emphasis on the atrocities of the convict period only to engage in another form of denial. Van Diemen's Land had been a place of darkness. In the end Tasmania had turned out to be no better. Leo Schofield, writing in the *Sunday Age* on 5 May 1996, described a bush walk in Tasmania, insisting that, during the walk he had 'felt that at some turn in the track, or emerging from an ancient forest of myrtles, I might be confronted with some inconceivable evil'.

The implications of this kind of thing, that Tasmania is somehow possessed by unspeakable forces, transform the island state from a microcosm encapsulating the essence of the Australian experience to a repository for evil, deftly excised from the fabric of mainland society, and transported, like the convicts themselves, to a suitably remote outpost.

The task of assembling a brief history of the penal settlement at Port Arthur is harder than one might expect. Some records have been lost or deliberately destroyed, others are not held at the Site or even in Tasmania. Philip Hilton, the Education Officer at the Historic Site, has worked for years with an assistant to build up a reliable database from the central collection of individual convict records, instituted by Lieutenant-Governor Arthur. Until this work is completed fundamental information like the number of men who were held at the prison or the number who died there remains uncertain. Figures cited by historians and tour guides alike are often informed guesses or simply fragments of legend, lifted from the past and put to curious new uses, like blocks of convict stone pulled from a probation station wall to prop up a gate. And, in this postmodern age, everyone knows how a solid fact twists in the hand, changing to part of a personal interpretation simply because one has selected it. There can never be a complete or impartial history of Port Arthur. Yet by assembling one account after another we can at least make some attempt to move closer to a clearer understanding, not simply of the past, but also of the present.

Before the American War of Independence the British had been in the habit of transporting a steady stream of convicted felons to their colonies on the other side of the Atlantic. Once these colonies had been lost, convicts were held in the hulks moored on the Thames while the British government settled down to consider whether transportation should continue and, if so, where the convicts should be sent.

The first question more or less decided itself. The crime rate was increasing, plans for two new penitentiaries in England had broken down, and the hulks were bursting at the seams. The need for some new repository for Britain's unwanted citizens was becoming acute. Almost every corner of the globe was considered: Lemaine on the River Gambia; the Cape of Good Hope; the East or West Indies; Canada; Algiers; Tristan da Cunha; the Falkland Islands: Madagascar . . . Eventually, in June 1786, the British government fixed on New South Wales, suitably remote yet favourably placed for the establishment of a future trading centre in the south-west Pacific.

And so, in January 1788, the First Fleet, bearing close on 1500 souls, more than half of them convicts, arrived at Botany Bay, not far from what is now the city of Sydney.

Five years later Governor King made up his mind to send a contingent south to the island of Van Diemen's Land, partly because he suspected that French explorers were about to claim the place for France, and partly because, like his masters before him, he wanted to offload some of his convict population to a spot that might, in the future, yield commercial gain. He had heard of plentiful timber in the southern island as well as abundant seals and whales, and fertile tracts of land which might be planted with wheat.

Once Van Diemen's Land had been claimed as a British colony it became, like New South Wales, an imperial gaol. By 1832 there were almost 12,000 transported felons on the island, all carefully organised into a series of classes according to a scheme devised by Lieutenant-Governor Arthur. In fine-tuning his system, Arthur became aware that punishment meted out to men in the lowest class, held at the penal settlement of Macquarie Harbour on the west coast, was proving too severe. Instead of being encouraged to reform and work upwards to a higher class and lighter penalties, convicts at Macquarie Harbour were falling into desperation and increased crime. There were cases of cannibalism when groups of escapees attempted to make their way through the dense bush that separated the gaol from the settled parts of the island. Or prisoners would murder fellow convicts simply to get sent back to Hobart and put an end to their own misery.

There were other reasons, too, for closing the prison at Macquarie Harbour. Hell's Gates, the entrance to the Harbour, had long been a danger to visiting ships. The cost of carrying provisions to such a remote outpost was disturbingly high. No food, apart from a few potatoes, could be grown in the bleak climate and inhospitable soil.

In 1830 Arthur turned his attention to a different site which seemed perfectly suited to replace Macquarie Harbour as a place of punishment for secondary offenders. This was the body of land south of the narrow isthmus known as Eaglehawk Neck: Tasman's Peninsula, a 'natural penitentiary' since any runaway, hoping to escape by land, must make his way along an exposed and easily guarded corridor. Here Arthur would place guards and later, thanks to the inspiration of a young ensign, a line of savage dogs.

It was clear, moreover, that the place was not attractive to free settlers. Very few, apart from a Mr Gellibrand, had shown any interest in it. Yet there were good stands of eucalypts on the Peninsula, so that, like Macquarie Harbour, it could serve as a source of timber for the colony. And it was, by sea, conveniently close to the capital and seat of government. A short voyage down the Derwent estuary and across Storm Bay would bring a ship to placid Norfolk Bay or to the long harbour lying between Cape Pillar and Cape Raoul.

Here, well up on the western shore, the new penitentiary, bearing the name of the Lieutenant-Governor, was to be established. To this site came the prisoners from Macquarie Harbour as well as another group who had been held on Maria Island off Van Diemen's Land's east coast.

Nowadays nearly everyone who travels from Hobart to Port Arthur goes by bus or car down the Arthur Highway, passing through a string of small towns interspersed with farmland and tracts of bush until the road runs straight in under the tall trees clustered around the entrance to the Port Arthur Historic Site. But during the convict period and for decades afterwards the highway to Port Arthur was the sea. The prison was laid out with this in mind. Convicts brought in by ship looked straight up the hill in front of them to the church as though their gaolers were anxious to remind them that a just but stern God was watching their every action and the uphill road to Him lay at their feet.

> *Over the years, since it closed in 1877, Port Arthur has been the subject of much misrepresentation.*
>
> — IAN BRAND

Originally the sea ran in to a point much closer to the church than it does today. Gradually the flat area at the foot of the slope was filled in and reclaimed so that a convict who had been released from Port Arthur and afterwards sent back for fresh offences would have found that, with each back sliding, the path to God had grown a little longer.

Naturally, it took some years to arrange this vista of exhortation. Early arrivals at the site were faced with nothing so imposing, merely a camp of tents and wooden huts. Sawn timber houses, barracks, workshops, a store and a hospital came next with more elaborate structures of brick and stone appearing as time went by. Along with the church, built in 1836 and 1837, came a guard tower, then a hospital for eighty patients, substantial residencies for senior civil officers. The Model or Separate Prison, a replica of the English Pentonville and expressive of the new theory that solitary confinement and silence were more conducive to reform than the cat-o'-nine tails, was built between 1848 and 1852.

Peter MacFie, who served as Interpretation Officer at the Site from 1984 to 1991, explains that by 1846, 'with a peak population of 1200, plus up to 1000 free people, including soldiers, officials and their families, Port Arthur was a prison town'. It was also 'virtually a self-sufficient industrial centre', producing, amongst other things, ships, bricks, cut stone, garden tiles, boots and shoes, iron castings, clothing, vegetables and massive amounts of sawn timber.

Life for anyone sentenced to a term at Port Arthur was not meant to be easy. Marcus Clarke in his novel, *His Natural Life*, published in book form in 1874, represents the place as a torture chamber, a hell on earth, but Ian Brand, who put together twenty-five volumes on the prison's history, claims that 'Over the years, since it closed in 1877, Port Arthur has been the subject of much misrepresentation. Phrases like 'brutal treatment' and 'savage punishment' are still commonly used in talking and writing about the penal settlement, and, as a result, visitors have received a distorted view of Port Arthur and the treatment which prisoners there received'.

It has also been argued that a Port Arthur man from famine-stricken Ireland or the slums of London had a better chance of staying alive and eventually leading a decent life than his counterpart back in Mayo or Seven Dials, though whether this says more about the British government's bungling and inhumanity in dealing with the Irish Potato Famine and poor relief at large, than about enlightened policies at Port Arthur is open to question.

Certainly, if the dietary tables issued by the prison authorities can be taken at face value, the men were not badly fed. There was a lot of bread and potatoes, an adequate ration of meat, occasional soup and green vegetables, tea, gruel, and suet pudding on Sundays. Some of the men and many of the young boys, held in a separate establishment at Point Puer across the bay, were taught trades. After supper in the evenings there were classes in reading, writing and counting. Ministers of religion, beginning with the Reverend John Manton, were appointed, as he put it, 'to preach the word of life to these degraded outcasts', although Manton seemed resigned to waiting until the Last Judgement to see any results. The success of his mission, he admitted, 'the great day alone will unfold'.

In the meantime some convict records suggest a degree of reformation, with individuals passing from hard labour to lighter duties as sub-overseers or gardeners, before moving on along the course to freedom. Once freed, the former Port Arthur inmate, no longer the subject of a government record, can be hard to trace unless, of course, he fell into crime again and was returned to prison. Yet some careers have been charted, including a number that the Reverend Manton would have found reassuring. George Greatbatch, for instance, sent to Port Arthur after twice absconding from chain gangs and 'stealing his irons . . . the property of the Crown', married five years after receiving his pardon, took up farming, and reared a large family all of whom, according to his son's obituary, united with the infant Church of Christ on the Tasman Peninsula.

As against all this other records create a very different picture. Many of the gangs at Port Arthur were worked in chains which Arthur considered as severe a punishment 'as could be inflicted on man'. Even if they were not chained, convicts might labour for up to twelve hours a day under daunting conditions, carrying massive weights of timber, breaking stone in the quarries or toiling up to their shoulders in water at the dockyards. Most feared was assignment to the Coal Mines at nearby Plunkett Point. Here men were held in tiny underground cells whose remains, looking much like brick-lined graves, can still be seen. They laboured day and night in eight-hour shifts and, according to Henry Fry, who visited the mines in 1847, were obliged to crawl along passages where the roof was too low to allow anyone to stand and the air so foul that Fry's party had trouble keeping their lamps burning.

In these conditions there was, as the Controller General of Convicts admitted, 'difficulty of maintaining complete surveillance over the men while at work' so that 'unnatural crimes', including, apparently, a good deal of male rape, were common. Through all this a convict was required to abide by a mass of regulations governing every action from saluting all civil and military officers to caring for his bedding and eating utensils. He could be punished for failing to place his cap and boots in front of his berth in a uniform manner or neglecting to fold his bedding according to pattern, for wearing his cap in the Port Arthur penitentiary or leaving his berth without permission from the constable on duty.

The records of many prisoners are a litany of punishments which can hardly be described as anything other than savage when set against the offences that had been committed. Thomas Sanders, for instance, was given an extra month's hard labour in chains for talking in church and, later, six days solitary confinement for having tobacco in his possession. George Britton was sentenced to three weeks in the chain-gang for sitting down during Divine Service and various periods of solitary confinement on bread and water for 'not giving his shirt to be washed agreeable to orders' or 'having some new rope yarn in his possession'. Later he progressed to batches of seventy-five or a hundred lashes for absconding, notching up a total of 766 stripes between his arrival in the colony and his death 'when setting fire to a blast of gunpowder' in the Port Arthur stone quarry.

Regulations in the Separate Prison were even more stringent. The strictest silence was maintained at all times; both prisoners and officers had to wear slippers so that not even a footstep could be heard; hoods had to be worn by all prisoners to prevent them recognising each other; in Chapel they were housed in separate stalls so that communication was impossible. On the wall of each cell was a longer list of rules, cautioning inmates not to read aloud or make any other noise whatever 'except such as may be unavoidable in the performance of their allotted work'; not to mark, deface or damage in any way their books or utensils or put their slates and copy books 'to any unauthorised purpose'; not to unroll their bedding before the bell had been rung for that purpose or have in their possession 'any unauthorised article whatever'; not to take down the lamps without permission or allow them to burn above a moderate height'.

Frederick Mackie, a missionary who visited the model prison in 1853, noted that, 'In case any man is refractory there is a dark, dumb cell in which he is confined for a time. Its stone walls are three feet thick, and the doors are double so that no sound can be heard without.' He went on to observe that confinement in the model prison produced striking effects: 'in most cases the strong man, the hardened criminal, was bowed down and broken in spirit'.

But there is something muted about Mackie's report, as though he harboured some latent doubt about the extent to which the routines of the Model Prison represented the progressive alternative to corporal punishment and the ready way to penitence that the system's Quaker champions had led him to expect. Could it be that the 'broken in spirit' had the look not of men brought to contemplate their misdeeds but of wretches who were being driven slowly mad?

It is hard to know how many of the 'lunatics' for whom the Asylum was built in the mid-1860s were directly affected by life in the Model Prison rather than experiences such as a stint on Norfolk Island. Despite Arthur's misgivings about overly severe punishment at Macquarie Harbour, Norfolk Island was maintained as a kind of nether hell for offenders who remained incorrigible in the face of the worst that any other penal settlement, including Port Arthur, could inflict on them. Some occupants of the Asylum may have been 'lunatic' before leaving Britain while others were undoubtedly senile.

After transportation of convicts came to an end in 1852, the convict population went on slowly ageing. Before long the system found itself encumbered by prisoners too old and infirm to do any but the lightest work and by a mass of free paupers—men who had served out their sentences or received pardons but had no means of support. Together the 'lunatics', 'invalids' and 'free paupers' hung like a chain of albatrosses around the neck of the authority that had shaped their lives, and by 1872 outnumbered the able-bodied convicts still held at Port Arthur.

Out in the bay, on what Reverend Manton described as 'a lovely little island about half a mile in circumference', lay another group of convicts who also made no contribution to the workforce—the occupants of the Isle of the Dead. According to the historian Richard Lord, 1769 convicts and 180 free persons lie buried here. Some eighty headstones remain to be inspected by tourists who come across on boat trips from the jetty near the Broad Arrow. There are soldiers from the detachments who mounted guard at the Neck, watched over stores, boats and work-gangs, marshalled prisoners to witness floggings and hunted escapees. There are civil officials, like the headmaster of the Point Puer school who died of consumption in 1843; several drowned seaman; a few elderly convicts for whom someone scraped up the price of a memorial; the wives of soldiers and officials; and, as in many nineteenth-century cemeteries, a large number of children. In the 1840s Catherine Mitchell, wife of the Superintendent at Point Puer, produced a graceful pencil sketch of the 'Isle de Morts' and wrote underneath: 'My first two darlings lie here, Francis Keast Mitchell and Henry John Mitchell—first 8 months, second 10 months old.'

Almost all the convict dead were buried in nameless graves, at first because their relatives were not allowed to erect tombstones and later, it seems, because only a handful of those who could be tracked down and informed that a son, a brother or a husband had finally perished, had either the cash or the will to demonstrate that he was still somebody's darling. There are nine convict gravestones on the Isle of the Dead and the records of the men who lie under them, along with what can be discovered about some of those in unmarked graves, shed a good deal of light on life and death in this prison at the end of the world.

Some records give no cause of death but three of the convicts with headstones, and perhaps as many as a third of those buried on the island died in accidents. Many of the prisoners at Port Arthur were men of small stature. Take any group at random and almost always more than half turn out to have been under 5'6" (165 cm), with some like John Jones, one of a party that made off with the Commandant's whale boat in 1839, measuring less than 5' (150 cm). A large percentage of this dwarfish population had grown up in the poorer parts of London or the slums of Britain's industrial cities and had had little to do with any timber beyond the floorboards and rafters of a thieves' kitchen. Set to bringing down some of the tallest trees in the world, and worked, often, in irons so that they couldn't run, one after another joined an inevitable procession to the Isle of the Dead:

> William Robinson, 5'3¾" (159 cm), a tailor by trade, tried at the London Quarter Sessions for stealing a coat, 'died 28th March 1833, crushed under a log of timber';
>
> Edward Coombs tried at the Central Criminal Court in London for stealing beef, 'died at Port Arthur from injuries received from falling of limb of a tree';
>
> James Forbes, a Scotsman aged 54 years, 'killed by falling of a tree at Long Bay Port Arthur 5th December 1866' . . .

And then, of course there were other men from the probation stations around Norfolk Bay, places like the timber-getting settlement at Cascades or the Coal Mines at Plunkett Point which had accidents and cemeteries of their own.

Some accidents have the feel of suicides. George Britton by March 1861 had assembled one of the longest of all the convict records, including fifty-three separate sentences of hard labour in chains. About a year after being returned to Port Arthur for the sixth time, when he 'came to his death . . . setting fire to a blast of gunpowder on a rock', he was apparently 'stooping over the said blast' so that he was struck in the forehead and instantly died. The case of Dennis Collins, whose story is recorded by the Reverend Manton is much clearer.

Collins had been a sailor, seen active service, and lost a leg fighting for his country. Having found a refuge in Greenwich

Hospital he 'violated the regulations of the establishment' and was dismissed. He applied for a pension and was refused. Not unreasonably he began to feel ill-used, went to the Ascot race-course and threw a stone at the King, causing William IV to cry out that he had been shot. In fact Collins had done no more than dent his sovereign's hat, but he was sentenced to death for high treason and ended by being transported for life. On arriving at Port Arthur he was given some 'light work, his age and general decrepitude exempting him from the more severely worked gangs', but 'declared his determination not to go through even that form of labour, saying that he had worked for the King long enough and that he would neither perform the King's tasks, nor eat the King's food any longer'. Collins then went on a hunger strike, rejected every attempt to dissuade him with 'a degree of steadfastness of purpose almost unparalleled', and died after three weeks. The terrible thing is that hardly anyone has heard of him. The last burial on the Isle of the Dead took place in 1893. Thereafter the people of the free village of Carnarvon, which had grown up among the old prison buildings, were laid to rest in a cemetery close to the new toll-booth.

But some of those who went to school in the restored asylum and went shopping at Gathercole's General Store and Bakery are still very much alive. They remember playing in the ruins where some of their forebears had been held prisoner, reciting the pledge of loyalty on Empire Day and, when dances were held in the Asylum building, sliding up and down the floor between dances in a mixture of sawdust and candle grease.

≈

Neil Noye, the Mayor of the Tasman Municipality, is an alert, dark-eyed man who, despite the strain of the past year still looks younger than he is. At sixty-four he has given up football for golf but has kept the spare, athletic build of a fast-moving rover. He is descended from Charlotte Noye, who was transported to Van Diemen's Land in 1831 for stealing a watch, and from her son, James, who took up land near Nubeena, on the Peninsula's west coast, after the prison at Port Arthur had been closed.

Neil and his wife, Kath, still run the farm established by Neil's great-grandfather and live in the house his grandfather built on the property. Together they have brought up five children and, through good times and bad, have managed to keep the farm going. Neil has worked on the land ever since he left school nearly fifty years ago. His record of community service is almost as long. He is an elder of the local Church of Christ and, over the years, has held office in a string of organisations ranging from the Junior Farmers' group to the Tasman Show Society, the District High School's Parents' and Friends' Association, and the Nursing Home Board. He has been a member of the Tasman Council for twenty-eight years, serving as warden (as the mayor used to be called) or deputy warden for more than half that time. Three years ago he became Tasman's first mayor.

Ever since 28 April, Neil has put in hundreds of hours to help his community recover from the effect of the massacre. Flung abruptly into the world of fax machines, mobile phones and media hype in which he has been constantly required to speak for the people he represents, he has kept himself sane by getting up at 4 a.m. to clean out his chicken sheds.

We have a Peninsula, with very little water, which is just about completely surrounded by water. Quite a hilly country with farm lands on the western side but on the eastern side we are very, very densely forested with quite heavy timber and very, very high cliffs. I think we've got some of the highest cliffs in Australia round Tasman Light. Our council chambers are situated in Nubeena, which is a little fishing village. In years gone by it was a thriving area with the fruit industry, but now it is more of a fishing village and the centre of the population where we have our services like the hospital, doctors, shops and that sort of thing. School. Police. But we only have a population of 2500 so we do only have one policeman in the area.

I feel that I've only got a loan of the land at home where we are. My grandchildren are the sixth generation to live where I live now and I feel I've got a duty to just pass it on to the next generation. My son will take over. That's something we have decided on. He'll take over, we hope. There's been some hard years. I mean, farming hasn't been easy at times, but we've ridden out the storms and come out the other end a bit ragged and torn but we've got through 'em. We had fifty acres of apple orchard and then England went into the Common Market and the apple industry started to slide and go downhill and we had to take the tree-pull. I had children at school in Hobart, which was a very expensive exercise but we rode the storm out. We've been in others besides, but there's highs and lows in all things.

I like it down here. I've travelled the world. I've been all over the world, all around Australia, every part of Australia. But I still think this is the best place there is to be. We've got clean air, we've got beaches, we've got good living. The people are so friendly and I think the friendliness of the people is one of our biggest assets—with our scenery. You get to know everybody. I know 90 to 95 per cent of the people here and they know me. We're friends.

I think we are getting over the 28th. I looked over the Dunblane situation and it worried me that they were still going in hills and hollows and they were having problems in places. I didn't think it would happen here, but it has happened. When the hearing came up that upset a lot of people and the community was—well you could feel the tension . . . I just felt that, you know, we've got to get on with life. Life's got to go on. Got to. That's just all there is to it.

On 28 April the people who gathered at the Port Arthur Historic Site during the course of the late morning would have seen little resembling either the prison town of the convict period or the neighbourly village which grew up in its place. A few, including some of the twenty or so staff members on duty that day, had come in along the side road that swings away west to Nubeena at the entrance to the Site, but most had driven down the Arthur Highway from Hobart. About two kilometres from the toll-booth an approaching visitor would have noticed buildings beginning to cluster along each side of the road: some private homes or farms, together with a number of weirdly eye-catching structures suggesting the approach to a carnival; the Seascape guesthouse, lying below the road near the upper stretch of the bay on which Port Arthur stands and looking, with its pink roof and frilly curtains, like the home of the Sugar Plum Fairy; the Fox and Hounds, painted in glaring white and black to resemble the beams and plaster of a sixteenth-century English inn; the tower supporting a blue-shirted bushman at the entrance to the Bush Mill; placards, signs saying 'Welcome to Port Arthur'.

The cars and buses slow down as they come level with the forecourt of the Port Arthur General Store. The store looks like thousands of others across the country, selling fast food and groceries, picture postcards and Pepsi. In front there is the usual patch of bitumen with two outlets on to the main road and the usual row of petrol bowsers. The traffic moves on towards the toll-booth. Buses go to the right window, cars to the left. On a sunny Sunday there may be a queue. Visitors wait in their cars, reading the notices.

One placard promises forty hectares of gardens and grounds, another gives a table of entrance fees. One in six cars turn back, their occupants baulking at the price of the tickets. Martin Bryant pretended in an interview with police that he did not have enough money with him on 28 April to gain entry to the Site; when, in fact, he bought his ticket, he complained about the price.

35

Two of his victims considered turning away but decided in the end to go on.

Once past the toll-booth the road runs downhill to a car-park, flanked on one side by a toilet block and information office. In the same line, but thrust forward to form the far end of the parking space stands—or stood—another building. Visitors climbing out of their cars on that Sunday morning saw a notice on its side wall: The Broad Arrow: Cafeteria—Souvenirs—Films—Clothing—Books—Hourly Processing.

Almost everyone who comes to Port Arthur for the first time is amazed at how beautiful it is. The view east across the bay to the Isle of the Dead, Point Puer and the huge, fleecy bulk of Cape Pillar, swept on an autumn day by cloud shadows and delicate golden light, takes the breath away. Here is the Tasmanian paradox, Paradise and Hell in one, which baffled the Irish political prisoner, John Mitchel. Writing in his journal before being transported to Van Diemen's Land in 1850 he damned the place as 'outer darkness', 'a land where men are transformed into brutes', but when he arrived he was enraptured by the 'golden-hued blossoms of the wattle, the ancient mountains, far-stretching woodlands' and the 'parrots of most glowing and radiant plumage'. 'In vain', he wrote, 'I try to torment myself into a state of chronic savage indignation: it will not do here.'

Always, as families and groups of friends, having parked their cars or clambered from their buses, start looking around them, you can see their surprise. They come expecting something macabre and find instead a scene that makes them exclaim and point in wonder. They take photographs of the seascape, the Isle of the Dead and the Commandant's House standing among the trees above the blue water.

Close at hand a second, larger car-park lies at the foot of a bank in front of the café. A road runs above it to the jetty then swings north to the site of the convict dockyard. Immediately in front of the point of arrival, next to the Broad Arrow, lies the Port Arthur oval, the area reclaimed from the sea, backed by the bulk of the roofless Penitentiary. Beyond that rises a green hill and a scatter of smaller buildings: a guard tower, the gaunt ruins of the hospital and a neat yellow cottage where John Mitchel's countryman and friend, Smith O'Brien, was once held prisoner.

Nearer the road that runs behind the Penitentiary stands a house built in the Carnarvon period, now used as tea-rooms, while away to the right, among thickly clustered trees, lie the Asylum and Model Prison. There are more trees, close by, on the right: an avenue of English oaks leading to the shell of the church, and others by the road that flanks the oval, where picnic tables and barbecues are set out. At the top of the slope, running south from the church, is a row of carefully restored cottages that once housed chaplains, medical officers, accountants and visiting magistrates.

Nothing in all this suggests hard labour. There is no sign of the workshops that once crowded the site, no trace of the prison farm, the forge, the tannery or the vegetable gardens. No hint of the dust, smoke and bustle of a 'self-sufficient industrial centre'. Still less is there any indication of the kind of punishment meted out in the days before the building of the Model Prison.

The flogging yard is not identified. Nothing brings to mind the peculiar viciousness of the Port Arthur lash, which Robert Hughes describes in *The Fatal Shore*, nor Commandant Booth's use of 'boxes like dog-kennels where the prisoner was chained, breaking stones from a pile in front of him'.

Between the buildings, some looking spruce and solid, others mere ruins equipped with railed walkways, stretches of barbered lawn, green and smooth as baize, smile in the sun. The gravelled paths are white and wonderfully clean. In front of the remains of the Government Cottage there is an elegant flower garden and if you walk up to 'Civil Row' you will find more flowering plants in the meticulously tended plots around each cottage. Some of these dwellings are open to the public and are furnished as they might have been when Port Arthur was a prison town.

> *In vain, I try to torment myself into a state of chronic savage indignation: it will not do here.*
>
> — JOHN MITCHEL

Yet, oddly, this early Victorian elegance, reminiscent of musical evenings and crinolined ladies embroidering by lamplight, seems more remote from the chain-gang and the dockyard than the village which replaced the penal settlement.

There is little sign of that village now. There are no school children down in the Asylum, no post office or pub, no general store and bakery. Instead the place has become a kind of park, looking rather like the estate of some eccentric eighteenth-century nobleman with a taste for follies and picturesque ruins. But on 28 April 1996 there were plenty of visitors there.

~

The story of how the free village of Carnarvon became Tasmania's premier tourist attraction begins long ago. Well before the prison was closed down it had become a place that notable visitors to the colony were taken to inspect. David Burn, dramatist and newspaper man, went there in 1842 and examined a display of escapees' boats and rafts that Commandant Booth had prepared. Later the English novelist Anthony Trollope spoke with John Barron, the convict gravedigger who lived on the Isle of the Dead, and found him 'a sober, thoughtful, suspicious man . . . not in the least afflicted by ghostly fear or sensational tremours'.

Almost as soon as the prison had closed, curious excursionists began to arrive by steamer from Hobart. As the buildings were sold off to private bidders and hotels and guesthouses began to appear, the number of visitors increased. There were guided tours of the Penitentiary, church, magazine, hospital and—for an extra sixpence—the Model Prison. Sometimes ex-prisoners acted as guides. Back at Eaglehawk Neck, an old Port Arthur inmate called Harry Winter would strip his back for a shilling and show you the scars left by the flagellator.

Why did he do so well at this? Why did the excursionists come flooding south in such numbers? There was sea-bathing, of course, and splendid air, as well as spectacular scenery. The bizarre rock formations known as the Blowhole or the Devil's Kitchen, the Tessellated Pavement or Tasman's Arch were all worth a visit.

But from the beginning these were only side-shows. Port Arthur was, and still is, the premier destination.

The attitudes to the past displayed by early tourists are strangely similar to those expressed by a wide range of people in the wake of the Port Arthur massacre. One extract from the

Hobart *Mercury*, describing a Boxing Day outing in 1889, ignores the existence of the convict period and seems to suggest that the only reason for going to Port Arthur is to draw it into the Age of Innocence by pretending that nothing untoward had ever happened there.

> Persons of all grades, but all on holiday thoughts intent, were to be seen wending their way towards the Argyle Street pier and by 8 o'clock the deck of the *Flora* was comfortably covered with pleasure-seekers. Forty-five minutes later the gallant boat was steaming away from the wharf, whilst the Garrison band struck up a lively air.
>
> After three and a half hours' good steaming, the water being like a mill pond, the holiday makers were landed at pleasant Port Arthur, otherwise Carnarvon. Shortly after the arrival of the vessel the sports, which consisted of foot races and chopping matches took place . . .

More common than this kind of determined light-heartedness is the pleasurable thrill, the recognition of horrors which belong to another time and have no connection with oneself. The tourist peeps, with a shudder, into the dark cell and hurries back into the sunlight, assured that he or she is different from and infinitely better than what has gone before. So 'Dorothy', in a published letter, supposedly written from an Eaglehawk Neck guesthouse, describes a visit to the former probation stations around Norfolk Bay and contrasts the 'prosperous-looking men and bright-faced girls' of her own time with 'the sallow, gloomy countenances of convicts and stern faced wardens' of 'days long past'.

Even after the fires which swept through Port Arthur in the 1890s, the steamers kept coming. Horse-drawn vehicles brought parties from Taranna or Eaglehawk Neck, while in 1913 passenger coaches started lumbering overland from Hobart and taking in a few scenic wonders before arriving at Port Arthur in time for a tour of the ruins and dinner at Barnett's boarding house. It hardly seemed to matter that the hospital and the Penitentiary were in ruins—perhaps their condition made them even more reassuringly remote, more firmly part of the grotesque barbarity of another age. And there was something thrilling in the reflection that one was being vouchsafed a look at an alien world that would soon disappear entirely. Percy Shearn, a schoolboy excursionist from the north of the state, felt that he would like to do some oil paintings of the remaining buildings because 'they would be so nice as curios and be very valuable in times to come when the places are all pulled down and there is nothing left of these relics of the old days'.

The people of Carnarvon, having come to terms with the past in their own way, had no objection to boosting their earnings by accommodating tourists. Fishermen tied up their boats and acted as tour guides for a shilling a time. The husband of the Post Mistress ran a freight and passenger service, and the village pub promised every attention to travellers. In all this, most held true to that recognition of the past as the ground in which the future is planted that lay at the heart of Carnarvon. They remembered the convicts as real human beings who had real ties with themselves.

In 1926 when it became known that a new version of *For the Term of His Natural Life* was to be filmed on the Tasman Peninsula, there was nation-wide alarm over the damage that might be done to Australia's reputation by reminding the world of the days of penal settlement, but when the film crew arrived at Port Arthur, the local people tramped in from every direction to dress as convict extras, haul ploughs and break stones. At the same time, along with the shopkeepers, carriers, carpenters and hotel-keepers, they made a tidy profit.

By this time, the state government, having sold as much of Port Arthur as anyone would buy, had entertained second thoughts and accepted the recommendation of its Scenery Preservation Board, that the Penitentiary, church and Model Prison, along with Point Puer and the Isle of the Dead, should be gazetted as reserves. But, for decades, this brought little change to Carnarvon or 'the Port'. Gradually, as timber-getting gave way to farming and fruit-growing, the place grew quieter. The school was moved north to Nubeena. Shops closed. People moved away. The government acquired more buildings—the Commandant's house, Smith O'Brien's cottage—yet remained content for the Tasman Council to manage affairs in its own backyard under the auspices of various branches of the Scenery Preservation Board.

Then, in 1971 control of the site passed to the National Parks and Wildlife Services. A Restoration Advisory Committee was set up. The bicentenary of white Australia was approaching, and the nation was seized by the desire to rediscover and refurbish its heritage. The pace of change quickened until in 1979, the State and Federal governments agreed to fund a seven-year program of research and conservation at Port Arthur, restoring as many buildings as possible to what they had been in the days of the penal settlement, and stabilising the ruins of several more. All through the 1980s millions of dollars were poured into this project, so that within a few years, Australia's most significant historical site had become an investment which was expected to yield a return, a business enterprise to be managed by a body who would know how to market the Site when the funding dried up.

The Port Arthur Historic Site Management Authority was established in 1987. It was made up largely of Hobart business executives and by 1996 included no representative of the Tasman Council and only one Peninsula resident. Its mission, set out in its Strategic Management Plan, was to 'promote an understanding by Australians and visitors to Australia of the important role of Port Arthur in the evolution of Australian society, while preserving the heritage values of the Site for the future. This will be accomplished through leadership in conservation technology and in the use of innovative, educational and entertaining interpretation methods'.

But as government funding dwindled away in the early 1990s, the most pressing concern of the Board was to raise money. The Site was sealed off so that all vehicles, apart from staff cars or trucks, could enter at only one point, and a toll-booth was erected at the entrance. The local community, already resentful of the way in which they had lost control of what many still regarded as their home town, now felt debarred from even visiting the place.

For a time a number of private businesses, including the Broad Arrow and the Frances Langford Tea Rooms remained, and local people could walk through a gap in the fence to visit them or make signals to the attendant at the toll-booth, indicating that they had a resident's sticker on the windscreen. But gradually the Authority has taken over the buildings and the businesses. Peninsula residents, some of whom went to school in the restored Asylum, feel ill at ease. They cannot play cricket on the oval any more or buy fish from the punt that was once moored to the jetty. If someone challenges them, what reason can they give for wandering about without an entrance-fee sticker on their lapel? The staff, in fact, would be unlikely to eject them because they, too, are Peninsula residents, some of them descended from early settlers or convict forebears.

Even before 28 April, many of the guides, gardeners or office workers felt the strain of divided loyalties. The Site provides employment which is not easy to come by elsewhere in the district, but everybody knows that a local wit has dubbed Port Arthur 'The Vatican', the state within a state. Some are not happy about the way in which the past—their past—is sanitised, slicked up and packaged as entertainment. The evening ghost tours are a handy source of income for a good many families but, in private, some guides express dismay about the trivialisation of the convict experience, the way in which the distance between the tourist and the men who laboured in chains has been extended and exploited.

All this seems trivial enough in the wake of the massacre, but it played a part in deepening and complicating the anger and sense of helplessness experienced by many of the people whose lives were changed by the events of 28 April. It constitutes another way in which the past invades the present and needs to be recognised before a better future can be built. It is part of the meaning of Port Arthur, centre of a community in crisis.

THE DAY

~

I think if I hadn't seen inside the Broad Arrow I'd be still wondering today what was there and I don't wonder any more. It's not real though. It's just like something I might have seen on television.

— COLIN DELL

At 1.30 p.m. on 28 April the green lawns and white paths of Port Arthur were glowing in the mild autumn sunshine. The garden in front of the ruins of Government Cottage was bright with flowers; the Isle of the Dead floated in a blue sea; the windows of the restored cottages twinkled with cleanliness, and the Penitentiary that Robert Hughes has described as 'an almost maternal ruin' had never looked more benign.

A fine Sunday always meant a good crowd at the Site. People had been coming and going all morning, and by now there were over 500 visitors inside the boundaries. A good-sized crowd had gathered outside the Information Centre, waiting for the 1.30 p.m. guided tour to begin. Meanwhile those who wanted to look around for themselves were moving about the paths and straying under the trees or over the hillside. Everyone wore a round red sticker to show that the entry fee had been paid. Most carried cameras. From the car-park next to the Broad Arrow, you could see small brightly coloured figures on the far hill pausing to take pictures. Others were picnicking at the barbecues near the oval or inspecting buildings like the church or the Model Prison. The Frances Langford Tea Rooms in the Federation-style Carnarvon house behind the Penitentiary was doing good business. So was the Broad Arrow where the staff had just got through the busiest part of the lunch-time rush.

There were about sixty people inside the building, most of them seated at tables in the restaurant section. Some were at the counter where three staff members were filling plates from the bain-marie and serving take-aways. Brigid Cook was hard at work in the kitchen behind the servery while, away to the right, Elizabeth Howard and her second cousin, Nicole Burgess, were on duty in the souvenir and gift shop. A handful of visitors were browsing among the display stands, fingering jumpers and T-shirts, selecting picture postcards.

[handwritten margin notes: Cook's friend; Leola's girls working in the shop]

The young man with long blond hair ordered a large meal and a can of soft drink, as well as a cup of fruit juice. He took his tray outside to one of the tables on the balcony in front of the café. Suddenly he remarked to the people around him that there were a lot of 'wasps' about. A little later he said something about the absence of Japanese tourists. According to Petra Wilmott, his girlfriend, this was not the first time Martin Bryant had linked these two topics so it seems likely that he was using 'wasps' not in reference to insects that plague picnickers, but as the well worn acronym for white Anglo-Saxon Protestants. He seems not to have grasped its full meaning, using it simply to mean 'white people'.

Certainly, what was to happen in the next few minutes suggests that there may have been a racist element in Bryant's thinking, that Asian tourists stood higher on his hitlist than white ones.

He ate quickly, gathered up his possessions, including a large blue bag and a video camera, and went back into the café. He moved towards the rear wall, stopped and dumped the things he was carrying on an empty table, near the north-west corner of the dining area.

Mick Sargent and his girlfriend, Kate Scott, who had both come from Perth to attend a wedding in Hobart, were sitting about two tables away with a friend, Caroline Villiers. The fourth member of their party, John Riviere, had just gone over to the servery to get something else to eat. Mick Sargent gave this account of what happened next:

I thought, 'What's he up to? Because he's obviously a tourist, or trying to look like one, then why is he carrying this big, heavy bag?' I thought that he was a real glutton for punishment, lugging that all over the place. I checked him out and he put the video camera down on the table and I looked up at his face and he was staring at me. I stared back: he seemed quite young, not as old as I later found him out to be. He was staring like, 'What's your problem?' and there we were, in this stand-off. It's hard to explain. It's like a male thing. We were sizing each other up and I could see in his eyes that there was something going on. I thought he was just pissed off because I was staring at him and we kept staring for about 10–15 seconds.

Then Kate Scott, who was sitting with her back to the man with the bag, said something to Mick and the stand-off ended. When he glanced up again, Bryant had turned away and was gazing at an Asian couple who were eating their lunch at a nearby table. Thinking nothing of it, Mick had just looked back at Kate when there was a loud explosion.

The young man with blond hair had produced an AR15 semi-automatic rifle from his sports bag and shot Moh Yee Ng from Kuala Lumpur in the neck, killing him instantly. A second later, before anyone could move or speak, he shot the second

Malaysian visitor, Soo Leng Chung, in the head. Mick Sargent saw the second shot fired Rambo-style from the hip, saw the gunman swing around and bring the rifle up to the shoulder, aiming straight at Mick. The third shot grazed Mick's scalp as he fell to the floor. The fourth brought Kate Scott down beside him, killed by a bullet fired directly at the back of her head.

For a few seconds Mick thought that he had been fatally wounded. He felt a burning sensation on each side of his head and blood running from his scalp. He could see that Kate, lying on her stomach beside him, was already dead and thought for a moment that it was good that they should die together. Then he realised that he was still alive and that the wound to his head was only superficial. The will to go on living flared up again, so he pushed his head under his girlfriend's body and remained still, hoping the gunman would think his third shot had claimed another life.

Anthony Nightingale, a loans manager with the Commonwealth Bank from Keysborough, Victoria, was sitting alone at a table near the front of the café, facing inwards. Apparently, when the shooting started, he jumped to his feet, leaned forward and shouted 'No, no! Not here!' Bryant turned and shot him in the neck.

At the next table, six members of a party of ten, also from Victoria, were just finishing their lunch. The Schadendorfs, the Broomes and the Fidlers had decided to eat while they waited for the last four people in their group to turn up. Kevin and Marlene Sharpe, Kevin's younger brother, Ray, and their friend Wally Bennett had just come into the café and were standing in a huddle talking to the early arrivals with their backs to the gunman.

What occurred next is unclear. People were starting to realise that something terrible was happening, and began to dive under tables, to thrust companions under cover. Kevin Sharpe may have turned towards Bryant and flung out his arm to protect his wife or pull her to the ground. He was shot twice, once in the arm and once in the head.

Walter Bennett was shot in the neck. Medical and ballistic evidence suggests that the bullet which killed him went on to strike Ray Sharpe, causing massive head injuries. Gary Broome, John Fidler and his wife, Gaye, were all hurt by shrapnel—fragments of one or more of the bullets that had killed people close by.

Perhaps it was at this point that Mick Sargent looked up and saw Caroline Villiers crouching in a corner. John Riviere, who had taken cover behind the servery counter, thinks that Mick called out, 'Keep down! Keep down!'

Mick has said that he was scared that Caroline would make a run for the door. He signalled to her and, when she joined him under his table, shoved her head, along with his own, under Kate's body.

Tony and Sarah Kistan, from Sydney, with their friend, Andrew Mills, who had moved down to Hobart only two months earlier, were lunching at a table just beyond the one occupied by the group from Victoria, towards the centre of the room. When the shooting started, the two men got to their feet, and Tony Kistan, once he saw what was happening, tried to push his wife towards the door. Both he and Andrew Mills were gunned down with single shots to the head.

Again, people close by were wounded by flying shrapnel. Peter Crosswell, Thelma Walker and Pamelia Law all worked for the Camp Quality organisation, founded to help and support children suffering from cancer. Peter Crosswell, who lives near Hobart, was an area co-ordinator, while his two elderly companions had come from the mainland to promote understanding of young cancer patients by giving puppet shows in Tasmanian schools. They had just started their lunch when they heard three loud bangs. Peter got up to investigate at the moment, it seems, that Bryant emerged from the back of the café to move in on the Sharpe brothers and Wally Bennett. As the men fell, Peter recalled that he 'jumped on top of the two women . . . and landed on the floor . . . told them just to lay dead still'. But, as Damian Bugg, the Director of Public Prosecutions explained at Bryant's sentencing hearing on 19 November: 'Thelma Walker and Pamelia Law . . . were struck with shrapnel or fragments from the shots which killed Mr Kistan and Mr Mills . . . Mrs Walker sustained shrapnel wounds to the right temporal region, to the back and right ankle.'

Pamelia Law felt a graze across the rear of her head and a stinging sensation in her right side. It seemed at first that she had been shot directly. Only later, when her wounds were being treated, did it emerge that she had been injured by shrapnel.

Pat Barker, who was sitting with her husband and a party of friends near the fireplace in front of the servery, also suffered injuries from shrapnel. Almost everyone at her table dived for cover, but before she could get to the floor, she was struck in the arm, hand and cheek by flying metal.

By now Bryant had moved into the middle of the room with tables crowded all around him, the front windows of the café on his right, the fireplace and servery on his left. Just in front of him was a group of three: Carolyn Loughton from

Ferntree Gully in Victoria, her boyfriend Graham Colyer, and her fifteen-year-old daughter Sarah. Bryant shot Graham Colyer in the neck, but this time, although he inflicted a wound that left his victim half-suffocated by his own blood, he failed to kill.

Next, he turned on a couple from Dunnstown, Mervyn and Mary Howard. Tucked away at their table in a corner by the door, they had been slow to grasp what was going on. Mervyn Howard was still holding his cup when he was shot in the head. His wife, shot once in the neck and once in the head, died beside him.

Under the next table, Joanne Winter was hiding with her father and one-year-old son, desperately trying to keep the baby quiet. Bryant was so intent on making sure Mary Howard was dead that he missed them and went on to where Carolyn and Sarah Loughton had fallen to the floor together. He shot Carolyn in the back, again failing to kill, then, despite Carolyn's efforts to shield her daughter, shot Sarah dead.

Robert Elliott and his wife, Alyece, were at the same table as Pat Barker. For some reason, which he could not explain, Robert stood up as Bryant went past towards the gift shop. Seeing the movement, Bryant turned and shot him twice, once in the arm and once in the head. He fell, badly wounded but still alive.

Meanwhile, outside the café, a couple from Corio in New South Wales were filming the Site with their video camera. Over near the Penitentiary, some two-hundred metres from the Broad Arrow, another visitor, Barry Turner, was doing the same thing. Both happened to record the sound of the shots coming from the restaurant, and both tapes prove beyond any shadow of doubt that the first seventeen shots were all fired within a space of fifteen seconds. Twelve people had been killed and ten injured in no more than a quarter of a minute.

Ian Kingston, the Site Security Officer and Manager of the Tasman Unit of the State Emergency Service, was standing in the upper car-park when the shooting started:

I didn't know what it was . . . I started running to the café. I didn't have a clue what was going on inside. The closer I got, I could see dust coming out of the walls of the building and I thought, 'Must be some wires arcing out in the walls or something in the ceiling.' Ran in the door. There was two bodies on the floor. I could see that they were dead . . . there was a lot of blood coming from them. I looked at the ceiling. Couldn't see anything wrong. All of a sudden the shooting started again . . . bang, bang, bang! I couldn't see where it was coming from initially . . . I could see one of the girls at the cash register. Her mouth was open. She was as white as a ghost and I thought she was looking at the wall, but what she was looking at was—in-between her and I was quite a few people, but amongst them was Martin Bryant.

The first thing I saw then was the gun come up. It was a massive gun, big magazine. And then he started shooting. He was shooting people right next to me, only half a metre away. The destruction of the bodies was unbelievable . . . How many were dead and how many were lying down, I don't know. I had time to think that I was going to die. I had time to think that I'd never made a will, that my children would lose their father . . .

The girl was still at the servery, still there frozen. And he's shooting people and getting closer to her and I'm yelling, 'Get out! Leave! Run!' In the finish, he shot a person only metres from her and she ran. She ran out the back door. Her life was saved by that. She would've been shot if she had stayed there. He got to a point where I could get out. I got out the door and with me I took as many people as I could, but the problem was that every person that was within a few seconds running from the café was flocking in. They were flocking in through the front door . . . probably 30 or 40 people trying to get into the café as I was trying to get people out, the ones that were closer to the door. I had to yell out 'Get out! Get out! There's a gunman in here!' They wouldn't move and in the finish I yelled out 'Fire!'

And then they started moving. I said 'Get out! Fire!' and they all ran. They thought there was a re-enactment going on.

The slaughter was not yet finished in the café. Over in the gift shop most people had realised they were in danger and were trying to find some means of escape. Three were sheltering behind a display table at the back of the shop. Two friends, Dennis Lever and Ron Jary from Red Cliffs, Victoria, managed to push their wives and another elderly woman behind a hessian screen with jumpers pinned to it. Peter and Carolyn Nash made for a door that led on to the balcony, but found it locked. Two staff members, Nicole Burgess and Elizabeth Howard, were still standing at their counter when they were shot down. Dennis Lever was killed next.

Ron Neander, who had just retired from an undertaking business in Adelaide, was on holiday with his wife, Gwen. He saw Mary Howard shot, and described how he and Gwen 'ducked behind a postcard stand, which kept us out of his line of sight'. But not for long. Once Nicole and Elizabeth had been killed, 'Gwen was the next one in line so she got it. Gwen was hit in the face. I knew straightaway she was dead, there was so much blood'.

Suddenly Bryant heard movement behind him in the café. He took a few paces back the way he had come and fired at Peter Crosswell as he lay under his table, still shielding the two Camp Quality puppeteers. The shot injured him in the buttock but did no further harm.

The destruction of the bodies was unbelievable . . . How many were dead and how many were lying down, I don't know. I had time to think that I was going to die. I had time to think that I'd never made a will, that my children would lose their father . . .

— IAN KINGSTON

Jason Winter was less fortunate. Just before the shooting started, the young winemaker from New Zealand had left his wife, son and father-in-law at their table by the window to carry the group's trays back to the counter. He had taken cover there with Dennis and Mary Olson, and must have been frantic with worry about his family, hidden from sight on the other side of the room. When there was a brief lull in the shooting after the killing of Gwen Neander, Jason leapt to the conclusion that Bryant had left the Broad Arrow through some outer door in the gift shop. He told the Olsons 'He's gone', and got to his feet. Bryant spotted him as he came out from behind the brick fireplace, in front of the servery and fired twice, killing him instantly. Dennis Olson, crouching nearby, was injured in the hand, chest, head and eye by shrapnel from those bullets.

Turning back to the gift shop, Bryant found Ron Jary, Peter and Carolyn Nash, an unidentified Asian tourist and Pauline Masters, a secretary from a Victorian medical centre, all crowded together by the locked door at the front of the building. He shot Ron Jary, Pauline Masters and Peter Nash, who tried to shield his wife's body with his own, and aimed his gun at the Asian, but by this time the magazine was empty. In less than two minutes he had killed twenty people and injured twelve. He quickly changed the magazine and left the café.

We can never know everything that occurred in those two minutes. A police taskforce spent months piecing together the accounts of the survivors, the reports of ballistic experts, the evidence of pathologists, measurements, tiny clues. As they worked, it became clear that what some witnesses believed to be true was at variance with most other statements and with the expert evidence. Some spoke, for instance, of Bryant 'moving backwards and forwards through the café' when it has been established that he went once through the building, only backtracking to shoot Peter Crosswell and Jason Winter, and then left by the main door. It may well be that other recollections of what was thought or said, of an arm flung out or someone pushed under a table have also been distorted by the confused rush of events. Yet even when only the hardest evidence is admitted several remarkable features of what happened in the Broad Arrow still stand out quite clearly.

Panic makes for dramatic scenes on film and good newspaper copy. The human stampede in which the weak are pushed aside and trampled has become part of the folklore of disaster so that we tend to expect extreme danger to produce a wild, destructive rush, like the one that turned Boston's Cocoanut Grove Night Club fire into a major catastrophe, back in 1942. Yet there was no wild panic in the Broad Arrow. As Damian Bugg stated, 'many of the people who were in the café at the time and survived to talk about it, spoke of little other noise than gunshot . . . the oppressive noise of the rapid fire of this gun'.

Five people ended up jammed together by the locked door in the gift shop, but the panicky stampede for safety, the screaming and clawing and thrusting away of the helpless, simply did not happen. Perhaps things went on so fast that there was no time for panic to set in, and yet that explanation won't quite do. People did react to the danger. A number of people pushed someone else out of the way, but never, it seems, to try and save themselves; it was always in an attempt to save another's life. Perhaps such behaviour is instinctive. If so, one can only say that these people had managed to live their lives in a way that kept their best instincts in remarkably good condition. They were generous, loving and brave and

They were generous, loving and brave and although many of them died, they demonstrated that, when put to the ultimate test, altruism is alive and well in late twentieth-century Australia . . . in a time when it often seems that selflessness is an outdated virtue, we owe them an immeasurable debt.

although many of them died, they demonstrated that, when put to the ultimate test, altruism is alive and well in late twentieth-century Australia. For that, in a time when it often seems that selflessness is an outdated virtue, we owe them an immeasurable debt.

~

The sound of the shooting inside the Broad Arrow carried across the Site. Peter and Noreen Wilson, who, at that time, leased the Frances Langford Tea Rooms, heard the noise. So did their seventeen-year-old waitress, Anita Bingham:

We were that busy and I was the only waitress working that day . . . Anyway, it was very hectic . . . There was Noreen in the kitchen who does the cooking and there was her husband and another boy in the bakery at the back and I think that was mainly it. Everything just seemed normal for the first half of the day until Noreen said, 'Quick, go and serve this bowl of soup.' So I was putting it down on the table to this foreign couple—Chinese or Japanese— and that's when I first heard the shots go off. Yes, and it just frightened me and this bowl of soup sort of just wobbled a bit and then people started to go 'Oh, what's that?' And one of my first reactions was that it must be some kind of a joke. Like, 'This is silly.' Because I'd only been working at Port Arthur for roughly three months before this happened. I really wasn't familiar with exactly everything that happened around the place. At first I thought there was probably a show going on, like mus- kets coming out or something. And people were just curious and getting up and going outside and we weren't sure what was going on and then when we looked out the window, we could see people ducking behind walls and cars and things.

MARKS STATEMENT →

← MY NEPHEW

Mark Kirby is a third-generation bricklayer from New South Wales who has lived on the Peninsula for about eight years. He had been contracted to do some repairs to several buildings at Port Arthur and that Sunday, was working on the front of the Penitentiary opposite the Broad Arrow.

Some of the brickwork there needed a lot of re-pointing and bricks needed replacing up to four storeys high. So to do that, it was decided that the Site would hire a cherry-picker from a hire firm in town. We'd been on that project—myself and Mick McMillan—he's the fellow that actually made the cross at Port Arthur. We were behind in our work program because I'd had an accident with this stone wall and dropped a massive great piece of stone on my finger and split it open and ended up with about three weeks off work. So we were behind, and the wet weather had got us behind as well so I was doing everything possible to catch up. I'd worked on Anzac Day.

I worked Saturday and it came to Sunday, 28 April. I worked through till twelve. The majority of the work I was doing was from the third storey to the fourth storey . . . I went over at lunchtime to the Broad Arrow and bought my lunch, spoke to the girls behind the counter in the food section. I was going to go over and say hello to Liz and to Nicole Burgess, but they were far too busy. So I left and went back to work. I got back to work at half-past twelve or thereabouts and elevated the cherry-picker up to about twenty-five feet from the ground, right in the corner where the clock tower meets the Penitentiary. It got to what I now know to be about half-past one. I was working on the corner and I heard the noises start. At the time, I didn't have any idea what was happening. But I knew there was something going on. There was something wrong. There was too much noise and too often. The series of what I now know to be gunshots was . . . it just kept going. I do remember a couple of slight breaks in it . . . There was so much noise, you couldn't put the thought to it being gunfire, if you can understand that. There was too much gunfire.

I've been shooting with blokes, gone on wallaby shoots and whatever and I've been in the bush when you've had twenty or thirty blokes around you with dogs running about and the whole bit and the confusion that it is. I'd never heard gunfire like this before. I'd never heard a noise like this. At the time my first recollection was that something was wrong with one of the gas stoves in the Broad Arrow.

And as I'm looking across to the Broad Arrow, Brigid Cook came around the back of the Broad Arrow and came running down to the side door. I knew it was Brigid. She had a uniform on with, like a sash across. I'd seen her an hour beforehand. She was very agitated. She was waving her hands around in the air. And at that time I knew there was something really wrong. For Brigid to leave the kitchen—there was something eminent [*sic*]. So I decided it was time I got down and went over and saw what was going on. So I started up the machine and started making preparations to get down from where I was, which is quite a cumbersome thing to do. You just can't press a button and then drop. Because of where I was, you had to retract the boom first and then do other manoeuvres to actually get out of position. While I'm doing this, I glance across to the car-park and eighty people in the car-park—I believe it was at least eighty people—turned and ran. I now know they were running for their lives. They ran across the car-park . . . they had actually been milling around in front of the Information Office getting ready for the half-past-one guided tour.

So they run, literally with the guides herding them along. You could see the guides over there. And they take off around the bottom corner by the toilets and start to run up the hill towards the toll-booth. So then I know there is a problem. There's something going on over there . . . At the same time, what I now know was gunfire was still going off and there are people—I can remember a fellow jumping, literally jumping over a fence in front of the Broad Arrow. He landed on the ground and just ran . . . I now know that at the time I started the cherry-picker Martin Bryant had walked out of the Broad Arrow. He lifted his rifle towards the eighty people who were running . . . and at that moment I started the cherry-picker. It's got a four-cylinder Wisconsin motor in it with basically no exhaust and as soon as he heard me start that thing up, he turned in my direction and fired two shots. We presume at me.

Other accounts tally pretty well with this, although some witnesses became confused about the time and, because things happened very quickly, about the sequence of events. It is quite clear, however, that the three staff members who had been at the counter in the café escaped into the kitchen while Martin Bryant was still in the Broad Arrow. They rushed out of the back door with Brigid Cook, who turned and ran west into the upper car-park to warn the people gathered outside the Information Centre. She says that she thought she might be making a big fool of herself because she hadn't actually seen any shooting, but since the three girls had made it clear that something terrible was happening and, like everyone else, she could hear the gunfire, she couldn't have been in much doubt. She must also have known that the gunman was likely to emerge from the Broad Arrow by the front door and yet, having tried to alert the crowd in the top car-park, she turned and ran straight across the line of fire from the door to warn people in the lower car-park. Like many other actions performed on that day, this act of extraordinary courage gives a heartening quality to an otherwise grim and horrific story of senseless carnage.

What happened in the next few seconds is difficult to determine. Those who had understood Brigid's warning were moving away from the café, but some, it seems, were still surging towards it and were turned back only by Ian Kingston's cries of 'Fire!'

Ian, who also acted with great courage and presence of mind, knew that he and the staff in the car-park had only a few seconds to get everyone out of the area.

He would have run out—anyone in front of the café he would have shot . . . We evacuated everyone we could get easily and quickly from in front of the café and in front of the Information Office . . . We hid them out of sight up Jetty Road, the road to the toll-booth. When we got up Jetty Road far enough, we took them into the Government Gardens (the area to the left of the road). We had them just at the corner of Jetty Road when Bryant came out of the café.

I'd only been working at Port Arthur for roughly three months before this happened. I really wasn't familiar with exactly everything that happened around the place. At first I thought there was probably a show going on, like muskets coming out or something.

— ANITA BINGHAM

At some point before everyone left the car-park Wendy Scurr, one of the guides, rang the emergency number 000 from the Information Centre. Not surprisingly, she had trouble convincing the person she spoke to that a gunman was wreaking havoc at Port Arthur and held out the phone so that the shots could be heard.

A few moments later Bryant appeared at the door of the Broad Arrow and—although Mark Kirby did not see this—fired once towards the crowd fleeing into Jetty Road. Ashley Law, another guide, heard the bullet whiz into the trees behind him. Then, as Mark has described, the gunman started shooting across the oval towards the Penitentiary where the cherry-picker's engine had just roared into life. The crowd rushed on towards the toll-booth. Some left the road with Ian Kingston, others ran into the bush on the right of the road and hid among the trees behind the Information Centre.

It's rash, to say the least, to speculate about what was going on in Bryant's mind, but it seems likely that at this point he realised that the AR15, deadly at close range, was not the weapon he needed for picking off victims at a distance. He left the café balcony, and went down the bank into the lower car-park towards his car, which was parked near the far end beyond a row of tour buses. In the boot of the yellow Volvo were two more guns: a semi-automatic .308 FN or SLR (self-loading rifle) and a semi-automatic Daewoo 12-gauge shotgun. The SLR was better suited than the AR15 to long-distance shooting.

By this time, Brigid Cook had run past the buses, which were all lined up with their cabins facing the café, warning as many people as she could, and had ended up near the back of the last bus in the line. As Bryant came along behind her, he looked towards the buses, spotted Royce Thompson, driver of the Tigerline bus, hurrying for cover, and shot him in the back. When he came to the last bus, a Trans Otway coach, he fired at Brigid Cook's group. The bullet passed through Brigid's right leg and entered her left one. Mark Kirby saw her slumped against a rear wheel of the bus and wondered what had happened. A little later another bus driver, Ian McElwee, helped Brigid along behind the back of the buses to a small sentry box at the edge of the oval and, using his knowledge of first-aid, attended to her injuries as best he could.

Then began a dreadful game of hide-and-seek in and around the buses. Yvonne Lockley and Winifred Aplin, on holiday from Adelaide, were running to take cover in their coach, when Bryant fired at them, injuring the first and killing the second.

Neville and Janette Quin, owners of a wildlife park on Tasmania's east coast, were trying to get away towards the jetty but doubled back when they found Bryant going in that direction. Bryant saw them, shot and injured Janette Quin, who fell close to the body of Royce Thompson. He then turned on Douglas Hutchinson, a passenger on the Trans Otway coach, wounding him in the right forearm.

At this point, Bryant finally reached his car, changed the AR15 for the .308 SLR and fired a few bursts across the water and back towards the Broad Arrow. Denise Cromer, who was standing near the boardwalk at the back of the Penitentiary, was startled to see gravel spurt up from the pathway only a metre or so away and marvelled at what she took to be a small explosive device, implanted in the path to lend realism to what seemed to be the elaborate re-enactment of a musket battle. There was more firing, first at Rodney Horrocks and Dennis Nudd, who were both sheltering behind a large tree on the upper side of the car-park, then at Pauline Sloane, who was helping the injured Douglas Hutchinson to safety, then at Janette Quin lying helpless behind the Tigerline bus. The last of these bullets found its mark, inflicting lethal injuries.

Next Bryant climbed up into the Red Line bus, and finding it empty, fired through the window at the Trans Otway coach on the right. Elva Gaylard was killed instantly in her seat.

Another Trans Otway passenger, Gordon Francis, ran down the aisle to try and lock the front door of the coach and was shot in the shoulder. Meanwhile Neville Quin, who had lost sight of his wife in the general confusion, started hunting for her. She was unconscious when he found her and her hands were cold to the touch. Suddenly he realised a shot had been fired at him. He turned, saw Bryant and ran to the front of the coach. There was a wild chase, during which the gunman fired again and again. Neville Quin managed to hide inside the coach but Bryant caught sight of him, followed and shot him in the neck.

'No one gets away from me,' said Bryant, but he had failed to kill his victim, who after a few minutes managed somehow to get off the bus and stagger back to his dying wife. Bryant took a shot at an American tourist, James Balasko, who was taping these events with his video camera, then got into the yellow Volvo and drove away.

By this time, Mark Kirby had reached the ground and shepherded a couple that he found on the oval into the shelter of the Penitentiary. He realised the danger they were in when he saw the splash of bullets in the water to their right. 'That was when I knew', he said, 'there was a nut in the car-park using a gun.'

Once inside the Penitentiary, Mark found a number of people who were preparing to go out and film the 're-enactment' but he managed to persuade them to stay where they were. He looked out and saw the yellow Volvo with the surfboard on the roof leaving the car-park. He heard more gunfire from the road to the toll-booth.

At that time, I decided Brigid Cook had been shot and I wasn't going to stay where I was while she was lying there, wounded. So I told the visitors to stay where they were and I ran across the oval to Brigid Cook, which I now think is probably the bravest thing I ever did in my life. At the time, we had no idea where he was. You could hear the gunfire getting quieter so logic put in your head that he was moving away, but I had no idea how many gunmen there were or where they were. So I ran across to the buses and Brigid wasn't where I'd seen her. She wasn't beside the bus, but there was a lady slumped behind the bus and a man who I now know to be Royce Thompson, under the bus. Royce was dead . . . Mrs Quin was in a very bad state. She was still alive and still lucid. She insisted that I didn't touch her. She said she was in a lot of pain.

With no first-aid training, I told her that I'd go and ring for help. I took off across the car-park. That was when I saw Brigid, who was injured in the leg . . . She was beside the sentry box . . . One of the bus drivers was with her and they'd put a tourniquet on her leg and packed it and stopped the bleeding. I then ran up to the Information Office. There was nobody there. There was nobody in the car-park. I didn't see a soul. So I went in and tried to use the phones in the Information Office and kept ringing four noughts and not getting anywhere and felt like a bleeding idiot.

Although Mark could not have known this, calls had already been made. After Wendy Scurr had rung 000, Peter Roche, who runs the ferry service to the Isle of the Dead, had also made a call.

Mick Sargent, having run from the café after Bryant left, had helped Caroline Villiers hide in the bush but had then gone back to the body of his girlfriend and had rung 000 from a telephone in the Broad Arrow. A nurse from Victoria, known only as 'Lynne', who later described how she, like Mark Kirby, made the terrifying journey across the open space in front of the Penitentiary, also put out a call for help before going into the café to do what she could for the injured. Also, Ian Kingston had left the guides in his group to lead the visitors up to the shelter of Civil Row, and had run ahead to the Old Parsonage to call the police and to start trying to co-ordinate some of the activity on the Site.

∾

Rural Tasmania is served by a network of volunteer emergency service units—ambulance, fire, the Red Cross and the State Emergency Service, which in its early years was used primarily for the clean-up operations that follow after disasters.

In the early 1980s the Tasman Peninsula SES unit initiated a change and, along with several other units in remote areas, was authorised to operate as a road accident rescue group. Since 1985, the unit has broadened its scope still further and now carries out marine and bush rescues, as well as extricating road accident victims from wrecked vehicles and dealing with other emergencies that cannot be handled by local police or ambulance officers acting alone. Members train regularly, simulating emergencies and gaining accreditation, not only in first-aid or navigation, but also in skills such as 'steep-slope rescue'.

Marlene Burton is thirty-nine. She looks cheerfully unconventional but reassuring, like someone who enjoys letting her hair down at parties but will always stay and help with the washing-up. She was born in northern Tasmania but moved south with her parents when she was only a year old, and grew up in a Hobart suburb. She has taken courses in women's studies, and metal fabrication and fitting and machining; lived in most parts of Australia; and worked as—amongst other things—a hairdresser and a clerk in a chocolate factory. She lives now with her partner, Ray, and two of her three children at Roaring Beach, an area popular with artists and alternative lifestylers, and works for PACE (Peninsula Action for Community Enterprise), an organisation set up five years ago to promote both a healthy economy and a 'rich cultural life' in the Tasman district. Marlene is President and Facilitator of the Tasman Co-op, one of PACE's recent off-shoots, which aims to assist people engaged in various small business operations such as herb-growing or toy-making.

At Delamere we were. It's another peninsula south-east of Adelaide. We'd been living on a big 800-acre bio-dynamic farm. That was a real eye-opener . . . There was a lot of potential there but when the house burned down we didn't have anywhere to live . . . I was very pregnant so I just wanted to come back to Tasmania and have a rest basically. That was pretty horrific—losing your house even though it was a rented house.

Everything that wasn't burned was fire-damaged in some way so we came home penniless and virtually assetless . . . I came down to the Peninsula because my sister was here and her family . . . and we used to come down here for holidays in the 1960s, camping near the Penitentiary. You could do that then.

It's a kind of odd-shaped peninsula . . . The west coast, which is where I live at Roaring Beach—it's pretty wild. We get the westerlies and southerlies blowing in there and that shakes the place up, lifts roofs off houses. Ruins gardens. Whereas on this side of the Peninsula where the PACE office is it's just picturesque with dozens of shallow bays, gentle green, sloping hills and agricultural land mostly. I like it here because it's a small population. It's clean. It's isolated. I like the people. There's a lot of potential down here. I think it just takes some visionary ideas to get people started . . .

Before I had this job, I had been working as a housemaid—this is after I started getting back into the workforce after Lewis was old enough to live without me for hours at a time.

And the housemaiding was nearly seven days a week and it's really hard work, so when I heard there was work at the Broad Arrow . . . I went along and talked to the manager and to everybody's surprise he asked me to start work the next day. I started out in the café, learning the ropes, you know. The slicing machine and washing machines . . . and when people are rushed off their feet, of course, it's first up who puts their hand up to make more muffins or scones or whip up some cream. So I was really enjoying my work there . . . I wasn't there on 28 April fortunately. Lots of the other girls were . . . I think the sentencing hearing was like a turning point because now . . . everything is out in the open. We don't have to listen to rumours and hearsay. We actually have the facts down on paper and everyone's read them. I think people are recovering . . . It's just, say, a matter of degree as to how much it's going to affect their life. We've all certainly been scarred by it.

It turned out I had to go to Hobart the Monday following the Sunday and of course, I went to hospital to see Brigid Cook, the chef at the Broad Arrow who had been shot in the leg, because she's my friend and my boss. It was very calm and kind of normal which I thought it wouldn't be at all. I suppose it was weird for me because it was so normal. Brigid was drugged up, I think, and waiting for surgery.

There was another friend there with her while I was there so it gave her friend a chance to get out and do some chores. I stayed with Brigid for a little while, gave her a couple of books I'd found at the bookshop on the way to the hospital. She had many visitors so I didn't feel like sticking around very long. I moved on and it just so happened that . . . another café worker . . . her niece had just had a baby a couple of days before at the hospital so I went over to the maternity hospital and checked

71

her out. Her friend was leaving to go back to work and had brought the wrong-sized bra so I rushed into town and changed the bra and came back . . . So it was just funny going in there to see someone who could very easily have been killed on the day but survived, and here I am visiting a new Peninsula baby. I've seen him since. He's doing really well.

On 28 April, Ian Kingston drew on his training and the experience that he had gained from a simulated emergency exercise:

The Unit had been called to a crash scene involving two tourist coaches. The resource availability and numbers of people involved were very similar and I kept referring back to this training scenario and to the checklist to make sure that I had notified all the relevant authorities. I coordinated activities on-site from when the incidents started until about 3.30 that day—for about 2 hours. That gave the police time to set up their forward command post at Taranna. It gave the ambulance service enough time to get their operations people from Hobart to Port Arthur . . . Once the police arrive, with an incident like Port Arthur, they automatically take control, seeing it was a crime scene. That's well and truly out of my reach . . . we're only trained to preserve a crime scene.

One great difference between the road accident on which Ian based his strategy and the reality he and everyone else faced at

Port Arthur was that repeatedly the Site was swept by fears of the gunman's return. After Bryant had driven away in his Volvo, Ian heard that the car had been abandoned at the toll-booth. He suspected that its driver had come back down Jetty Road on foot. After talking by telephone to the police from the Parsonage near the church, Ian had to get back to the café located a few hundred metres away.

> I was petrified that any second he was going to jump out from behind a tree and shoot me—getting from the Parsonage back to the café was the most fearful time in my life . . . Where was he? Was he there? It was dead silent. I could hear a little bit of activity at the café, but nothing much. So I ran back down, dodged from tree to tree in case he was still lurking on site with a gun. I finally got back. Went to the café. Couldn't believe what I'd seen . . .

By now, the realisation that there was a gunman on the loose was spreading across the Site. Staff were doing all they could to reassure and protect visitors. Members of the public with first-aid training, doctors, nurses and off-duty policemen were coming forward to help. Mark Kirby found two elderly women wandering in the car-park and got them under cover. He took calls from staff stationed in the Commandant's and Junior Medical Officer's houses:

> I said, 'Keep everyone inside. There's been a shooting down here . . . Lock the doors' . . . Finally, people started arriving. Wendy Scurr came from the Broad Arrow asking

for the first-aid kit . . . I went looking for it and I couldn't open the bloody door . . . A couple of minutes later Paul Cooper came from the avenue of trees round through the car-park with a first-aid kit in his hand . . . I could've run down and kissed him.

On the other side of the oval, Peter Wilson had warned everyone in the Frances Langford Tea Rooms to stay under cover. He had discovered that at least ten people had been killed in the shooting. As Anita Bingham put it:

I was just in shock. There were children and all in there—babies—and people were really scared. There were a lot of elderly people there too. We were basically instructed to keep them inside and calm down. And there was lots of talk . . . Noreen said 'You've got to keep them going'. It wasn't a time when we could just sort of sit down and wait till everything's over.

I had to keep getting coffees, get everything ready as quick as we could, just keep giving people tea . . . We could hear shots still going off. We didn't even know where this person was either, which was the scariest part . . . Then as time went by . . . people were safe to leave in groups and go further over to the museum . . . at that time I had all these coffees in my hand. I walked into a room and went to give them to people and no-one was there. All we could do was just clean up. It was just like I had to keep working like any other normal day.

∼

Just before the crowd of eighty or more visitors had gone running up the road that led to the toll-booth, a small party had set out ahead of the main group, but instead of sheltering in the bush behind the Information Centre or making for Civil Row they carried straight on up the hill. There were seven people in this group: four mainland visitors, John and Caroline Boskovic with their friends Peter and Pauline Grenfell, who had just finished lunching at the Broad Arrow, and a mother with two small children: Nanette Mikac and her daughters, six-year-old Alannah and three-year-old Madeline. The Mikacs lived at Nubeena, where Nanette and her husband Walter ran a pharmacy. Like many other locals Nanette also had a part-time job at Port Arthur—she was one of the ghost-tour guides who led parties around the Site each night, telling stories of mysterious happenings and apparitions. She was much attracted by the beauty of the place and had taken her children there that Sunday to enjoy a picnic in the sunshine while Walter went off for a game of golf at the club a kilometre or so beyond Port Arthur.

Nanette, with Madeline in her arms and Alannah trotting at her side, hurried ahead with the Boskovics while the Grenfells followed behind. They could hear shooting as, down in the lower car-park, Bryant ranged about among the buses. No doubt they were relieved to come within sight of the toll-booth, to feel that they were getting away from the Site. Nanette said to Alannah, 'We're safe now, Pumpkin'. When they heard the car coming up the hill behind them, Nanette obviously thought help was at hand. She moved towards the car when it stopped opposite her, probably expecting the driver to take her group to safety.

John Boskovic, who was a little ahead by now, turned back with the same idea. He saw Bryant get out of the car and put his hand on Nanette's shoulder, which was natural enough, but then to his astonishment he heard the blond-haired man tell Nanette three times to get down on her knees. She said, 'Please don't hurt my babies'. Then Peter Grenfell shouted 'It's him', and John Boskovic saw the gun in Bryant's right hand.

Nothing could be done to save the Mikacs. The Boskovics, the Grenfells and a third couple, the Duttons, who were close by, could only run for their lives. Nanette and Madeline were shot at point-blank range. Alannah was chased and killed when she left the road and tried to hide behind a tree.

A few moments before the slaughter of the Mikacs, two cars had drawn up at the toll-booth. Although Aileen Kingston, who was on duty there, had heard shots, she had no way of knowing what had happened in the Broad Arrow or in the lower car-park, so she took the entry fees in the usual way. The first car, a gold BMW, belonged to Ken and Mary Rose Nixon from Crabtree in the Huon Valley. The Nixons were entertaining three friends from northern New South Wales: Jim Pollard, Robert Salzmann and his wife, Helene.

If you live in southern Tasmania and have visitors from the mainland, a day out at Port Arthur is more or less obligatory, so Mary Rose Nixon had brought her three guests to the Site for the afternoon. Just behind the BMW was a red Holden Commodore containing a New Zealand couple called Buckley. The two cars had only gone about 100 metres down the entrance road when a man appeared in front of them to warn them there was a gunman on the loose. The Buckleys promptly backed up and turned round. Jim Pollard, who was driving the Nixons' car did the same, ending up just beyond the toll-booth, facing the Highway.

The Buckleys parked at the side of the road and got out to ask Aileen Kingston what was happening. As they were speaking, the three looked back down the hill and, to their horror, saw Bryant in the act of shooting Nanette and Madeline Mikac. The Buckleys had no time to get into their own car. They raced out to the main road, where they were picked up by Keith Edwards and his wife, June. Aileen Kingston took cover in the toll-booth. Martin Bryant, having murdered Alannah, drove on and parked close to the BMW.

Mary Rose Nixon's party were still in their car. Since Jim Pollard had turned it around, they had probably not seen the Mikac killings and must have been baffled as to what was going on. Later, in an interview with two police officers, Bryant gave a wildly inaccurate account of his actions on 28 April, but admitted to taking a BMW from its driver: 'I was in the Volvo, I stopped the car on the corner, there was a nice-looking BMW and I asked them to get out of the car . . . "Hey mate, can you get out, out of your car please, I'm gonna take your car"'.

This, unlike almost everything else Bryant had to say in that interview, may have been true. Certainly, when Debra Rabe turned off the Arthur Highway to enter the Site, she saw Bryant and Robert Salzmann arguing between the two cars. She also saw Mrs Nixon, who was in the front passenger seat of the BMW, signalling to her to go back. Then Bryant took his .308 SLR out of the Volvo and shot Robert Salzmann.

Jim Pollard, who was over seventy, got out of the BMW's driver's seat and, with great gallantry, walked around the front of the car to confront Bryant. He, too, was shot dead. As Debra Rabe reversed her vehicle towards the main road, the gunman finished his sweep of the BMW by killing both Helene Salzmann and Mary Rose Nixon and pulling their bodies out on to the road. Then he moved some of his property, including two pairs of handcuffs, the AR15 and some ammunition from the Volvo to the BMW.

Yet another car arrived at the entrance to the Site—a maroon Magna driven by Graham Sutherland. As they came towards the toll-booth Graham Sutherland, his wife Stephanie and their sons, Thomas and Stuart, were appalled to see bodies lying in the road and the way blocked by the BMW. Thomas shouted, 'There's someone running back to the other car!' It was Bryant, who grabbed the SLR and fired it at the Magna's windscreen, but by this time the Sutherlands were reversing at top speed. Although sprayed with glass, none of them was injured.

By this time, the service station and shop just north of the Site entrance was in something of an uproar. Keith Edwards was trying to stop any cars heading for the toll-booth; Debra Rabe and her passengers had driven in with news of the murder of the occupants of the BMW; and Jim Laycock, who had looked out of the door of his photo shop opposite the general store a few moments before, had seen Bryant dumping the bodies of Helene Salzmann and Mary Rose Nixon on the ground. Then the Sutherlands arrived with their smashed windscreen, issued another warning and drove on, quickly followed by Debra Rabe. Again, everyone involved behaved with great courage, stopping to issue warnings before trying to save themselves.

Glenn Pears, a young Tasmanian lawyer who had moved to Sydney, was visiting Hobart to attend his sister's birthday party. He was taking the opportunity to show some of the local sights to Zoe Hall, another lawyer, who had made the trip with him. From behind the door of his shop, Jim Laycock watched as Bryant arrived at the service station and blocked Glenn Pears's path as he was about to drive off in his white Corolla.

He just blocked their exit and then pulled or forced the man out of the car and threatened him with the rifle. The guy was saying, 'Don't shoot, don't shoot. Everything's OK.' Then the gunman yelled at him to get in the boot . . . then slammed the boot and he just went and shot the woman. It was the quickest shot, she just went. It smashed the window, went straight through, straight in the heart . . . It was the most frightening two minutes of my life, but at the time you don't think about that.

With Glenn Pears trapped in the boot of the stolen BMW, Bryant drove on again, back towards the Seascape guesthouse. At this stage, only he knew that the owners of Seascape, David and Sally Martin, were already lying dead in the house they had renovated together. He had killed them on his way to Port Arthur, because, it seems, they had refused to sell him a small farm they owned.

~

John Rooke was driving slowly towards Port Arthur, towing a loaded trailer. Suddenly a gold BMW, racing up the Arthur Highway towards him, swung across the road and came to a halt at the entrance to Seascape. A young man with long blond hair got out of the car, pointed a rifle at John Rooke's Datsun and fired two shots. Nothing happened. The bullets seemed to be blanks.

The occupants of the next vehicle were not so lucky. They were Linda White and Michael Wanders from Melbourne, driving along in an aqua four-wheel drive Holden Frontera. Linda slowed down, impressed by the sight of Seascape, set in its garden by the water. She noticed Bryant and his gun but imagined he must be hunting rabbits—until he lifted the rifle and fired it directly at her. The bullet struck the bonnet of the car and smashed part of the windscreen, sending a shower of glass up into Linda's face. Two or three more shots slammed into the car, smashing the front windows and shattering the whole of Linda's right forearm. She tried to drive on but, just round the next bend, the vehicle stopped. Michael Wanders, who had not been wounded, took the wheel, but because Bryant's first shot had cut the Frontera's throttle cable, his desperate efforts to get the car moving came to nothing.

Behind Linda and Michael's car, a maroon Ford Falcon sedan was approaching Seascape. Doug Horne was driving with Neville Shilkin beside him. Their wives, Faye and Helen, were in the back seat.

'He's got a gun!' shouted Neville Shilkin. At the same moment, a bullet smashed into the Falcon's windscreen and fragmented, wounding Doug in the chest, shoulder and right arm. Dazed and bleeding, Doug drove on, stopped, started again and finally pulled up in front of the disabled Frontera. Michael Wanders and Linda White came running towards the Falcon, expecting at any moment to be shot in the back. They scrambled into the car and Neville Shilkin quickly drove the whole party to the Fox and Hounds.

The next car to come down the Arthur Highway was a pale-coloured Magna, driven by Anne Wardle. As she came round the bend to the north of Seascape, she and her three friends were just in time to see Bryant fire at Doug Horne. With remarkable presence of mind Anne slammed her car into reverse, swung over to the opposite side of the road and backed away from the gunman as quickly as she could. Bryant took aim and managed to hit the Magna's windscreen but none of the occupants was hurt.

Simon Williams, a Canadian Embassy official from Canberra, on holiday in Tasmania with his wife, Susan, was startled by the sight of the Magna reversing towards him on the wrong side of the road. Almost at the same moment, he noticed Bryant by the roadside and heard a gunshot. He decided to go towards Port Arthur rather than back, but before he could speed to safety a bullet smashed through the two front windows of the Williams' red Falcon. Susan Williams was wounded in the head, and both she and her husband suffered serious hand injuries. They too went on to take refuge at the Fox and Hounds.

After this, Bryant apparently tired of shooting at cars, drove the BMW down to Seascape, took Glenn Pears inside the house and handcuffed him to something immovable, like the newel post at the foot of the stairs. He then took his AR15 and FN rifles out of the vehicle, doused the BMW with petrol from a can he had fetched from the Volvo and set it alight. He went back into the house and at some time in the next few hours shot and killed Glenn Pears.

By this time Nubeena policeman Constable Paul Hyland and Constable Garry Whittle from the small town of Dunalley at the head of the Forestier Peninsula had been called by radio to Port Arthur. They were out at Saltwater River, in the Tasman Peninsula's north-west, when the message came through, and drove rapidly in their separate cars back along Saltwater River Road. At Nubeena, which was on their route to Port Arthur, they picked up a further message, warning them to look out for a yellow Volvo with a surfboard on the roof-rack.

They decided to split up, one travelling on through Nubeena to the Site, the other going back through Koonya to the Arthur Highway. Paul Hyland went the long way round, taking in more messages as he drove: he was to look out now for a gold BMW, and there were reports of shootings at or near the Fox and Hounds.

Just past Seascape he saw an aqua Frontera with its front windows smashed, then another damaged vehicle outside the hotel. After speaking to some of the witnesses sheltering inside, he went back towards Seascape, and as he drove along, found that Garry Whittle had come up behind him. The two constables looked down and saw black smoke billowing from a car parked near the Seascape guesthouse and a figure running past one of the cottages set out around the main building. They decided to set up a road-block, with Paul Hyland warning all south-bound traffic and Garry Whittle stopping any vehicles coming up the highway from the direction of Port Arthur.

Two more police constables, Pat Allen and Perry Caulfield from the Hobart Accident Investigation Squad, came speeding by in a station-wagon, just as Garry Whittle, who had heard the BMW explode, was crouching behind the back of his car. Pat Allen explained: 'I shot down past where Garry was and went to the Fox and Hounds. I dropped Perry, gave him half a box of ammo and said, "Good luck".' Then he drove back to help Garry Whittle:

> As I was approaching Seascape, I thought, 'My big boof-head's on the right side to get shot.' So I did a U-turn in the middle of the road and started backing down the road, so my head was on the other side of the car. Then shots opened up and Garry ran into the ditch. I just kept reversing and another two shots went off—he was shooting at me, there's no doubt about it. I drove up to where Garry was, grabbed the walkie-talkie and bundled out next to him in the ditch.

Inside Seascape was a collection of guns and ammunition belonging to David Martin or his sons, so that Bryant now had access to a formidable armoury, including the two semi-automatic weapons he had taken with him into the house. Using now one weapon, now another, the gunman kept the two police officers pinned down in the ditch for about eight hours. Once Pat Allen stuck his head up:

> It was coming towards dark and someone on the radio said that they'd seen him on the roof and they needed to identify him. They needed to ID him so they could kill him if they had to. They gave me the option to stick my

head up and I did. I went to have a look under the wheels, to have a look at Seascape to see if I could see him and a shot went through the bumper bar and bounced somewhere on the road. He knew where we were . . . I thought about writing a note to my wife. Just in case. I thought I was going to die on and off from about an hour after I got in the ditch to an hour or so after dark. Then I thought 'Oh jeez, I'm going to get through this.' So you develop some determination.

Eventually two members of the Special Operations Group (SOG) joined the two men trapped in the ditch and managed to lead them to safety. That was not until about 10 p.m., by which time the largest police operation in the history of Australia had been underway for some eight hours.

Luppo Prins, the Tasmanian Assistant Commissioner of Crime and Operations, had received a call from the police radio room just after 1.35 p.m. He was told that seven people had been shot dead at Port Arthur. He put the Duty Inspector, Peter Wild, in charge of the situation, directed that the major incident room should be activated and authorised deployment of the SOG. Then he drove as quickly as possible to headquarters, listening in disbelief to reports of a death toll that climbed, as he drove, from seven to fifteen. Once he arrived in the major incident room, calls were sent out to Superintendents needed to take up positions like forward commander or senior operational officer; specialist groups such as the hostage negotiation unit, CIB, forensic services, communications, search and rescue, ballistics and coroner's clerks; the Premier, the Duty Minister, the

Minister for Police and Emergency Services, the Police Commissioner and Deputy Commissioner; ambulance, fire and the State Emergency Service.

In a suburban house close to the river Derwent, a police officer I will call 'Brendan' was doing his ironing and watching the football when:

I got a phone call saying I had to go to work. I'd heard a news report saying that I think it was ten people had been shot at Port Arthur and I thought 'Oh yes, doesn't sound quite believable.' But I had a phone call shortly afterwards, saying to get to work and I was going to Port Arthur.

It took a while for that to hit home, but I got to work and there was not total panic, but a bit of disorganisation—and that's probably sounding a bit harsh, too. Initially in a major crisis like this there is a bit of disorganisation before the wheels get into motion . . . We were told to arm ourselves and get our folders because we would be going to Port Arthur because there'd been a shooting. Reports of how many people were dead were a bit sketchy but they ranged from ten to fifteen and twenty-odd injured . . . The majority of us travelled as far as the Devil Park at Taranna where a lot of other police people were. There was a sort of semi-roadblock being set up to stop people going into the area and checking people as they came out. And media hounds were there, all over the place, as were my senior members, senior officers . . . superintendents and people who'd come out of the woodwork from everywhere. Later that night, we travelled into Port Arthur through the back way, through Koonya to the motel where we met again.

By the time Brendan arrived at the motel perched on the hill behind Civil Row, dozens of police were at work at Port Arthur, while along the Arthur Highway, at Seascape, the SOG were doing their best to ensure that Bryant had no way of breaking out of his refuge. At every stage they had been hampered by difficulties. Because of its remote location in a natural amphitheatre, Port Arthur has poor radio communications, so that police had trouble making contact with each other and at one point had to use runners. The Arthur Highway could not be used to get through to the Fox and Hounds or the Site because Bryant was shooting across the road at the constables trapped in the ditch. There was little cover around the house so that a direct attack by the SOG would have put more lives at risk. Nobody, apart from Bryant, knew at this stage whether the Martins and Glenn Pears were alive or dead, which meant that police had to act as though they were dealing with a hostage situation. In the end, they decided to play a waiting game. A negotiation team, led by Sergeant Terry McCarthy, spoke with Bryant on and off for over six hours until the Martins' cordless phone went dead because the gunman failed to recharge it. Through the night SOG members, backed by reinforcements flown in from Victoria, kept watch. Finally, after smoke was seen rising from the house, Bryant rushed out and stripped off his burning clothes. At about 8.25 on the morning of Monday, 29 April, Martin Bryant was arrested.

F elicity Langley creates an immediate sense of keen-
ness and force. She is the grand-daughter of George
Clarke, who established a farm near Nubeena in the
1880s and went on to become a stipendiary magistrate, coroner and warden of the municipality. She and her three sisters,
all of whom have returned to the Peninsula after living elsewhere, spent a great part of their girlhood on their grandparents'
farm. Felicity explains that she is 'regarded locally as a sort
of hybrid because I spent a large percentage of my life away
but most people knew me as a child so it puts me in a slightly
privileged position'.

In the 1950s she trained as a nurse in Hobart, travelled to
Britain and then took a job in Uganda. There she met and
married Michael Langley who later became a regular army
officer. In 1985, after leading the nomadic life of a service
family, the Langleys settled permanently on the Peninsula, the
place which their three children—though now scattered again—
have come to regard as home. The Langleys bought land within
sight of George Clarke's farm, built a large stone house with
stones collected from their property, and established a flower-
growing business. Michael is a member of the Board of the
Port Arthur Historic Site Management Authority and served first
as an Executive Director assisting the General Manager in
coping with the aftermath of the massacre, and later as head of
a Special Management Team. Felicity is a past president of the
Country Women's Association (CWA), a member of the Nursing
Home Board, and the organiser of the annual flower show.
She has assisted the recovery process through her work for

the CWA and her membership of a Community Link Group set up to disseminate information and provide support for people suffering from the effects of the events of 28 April.

On that Sunday afternoon, the Langleys were on their way to an Anglican Church service, which was to have been held at the Site. They arrived at the entrance only minutes after Bryant had murdered seven people near the toll-booth, shot Zoe Hall at the service station close by and forced Glenn Pears into the boot of a stolen BMW. Felicity became one of a small group who directed traffic to safety while gunfire could still be heard from the direction in which the gunman had disappeared, and nobody knew whether he would return.

Much travelled, Felicity compares the Peninsula to other parts of the world. She finds it similar to Washington State or Oregon: 'Hills. Water. Isolation. Narrow roads. Depressed areas. Translate the eucalypts to conifers . . . Timber industry'.

She lived for a time in Queensland, on Mount Tambourine, but prefers the Peninsula because it is free of the type of tick which, in Queensland, killed her cats and dogs, and of the type of developer who had begun to surround her Mount Tambourine property with new housing. And also she likes the climate: 'Mike says he likes four seasons and I agree with that . . . It's nice to have the water here as well'.

Mike was regular army and, no matter what, you have to retire at fifty-five. If you get to be Chief of the General Staff you still have to. So we were looking at where we were going to retire. I refused to have anything to do with the decision about buying down here because I didn't want to have it put upon me in later years that 'We never would have come here if it hadn't been for you.' And, in fact, we just made a couple of idle enquiries and somebody said 'Oh George Armstrong, who had been the medical officer down here, had some land and he might be interested in selling,' and we contacted George and he was interested in selling so, you know, we bought that just like that . . . We cleaned out the old house which had been used as a hay-barn and cattle-shed and what-have-you. And we literally scraped cow dung off the walls and floors. Major job. The place was water-tight. It didn't leak but it wasn't wind-tight. So we gradually patched that up and when Mike retired in 1985 we came down here and we lived in that little slab cottage for six-and-a-half years. One cold water tap. One old fuel stove that either burned or didn't burn. It had absolutely no draught control or anything like that. And we survived . . . People look and say, 'How can you live with these bare concrete floors in this new house?' In comparison it's Paradise.

I'd always had the idea of growing flowers. You know, as a service wife you never get the chance to do anything of your own. By the time you've got the family settled and organised and start looking for a job, you start thinking about the next posting. So that's one of the things you just have to accept . . . that you can have no career of your own. And so I'd always muttered about growing things and that's what we now do. I grow peonies and protea . . .

The massacre changed the lives of everyone involved. Unless they can develop themselves in another aspect of their life, for some people 28 April was a stage when their development came to a halt. But most people do. Most have accepted that their lives are different and are moving on.

The firing of Seascape resulted in a charge of arson, the last of a list of seventy-two charges brought against Martin Bryant: thirty-five counts of murder as well as others of attempted murder, aggravated assault, wounding, causing grievous bodily harm and unlawfully setting fire to property.

While the police and, subsequently, the Director of Public Prosecutions and the judge who sentenced Bryant presented a carefully connected account of his rampage, each crime was investigated as thoroughly as if it had been a single occurrence and Bryant's responsibility established beyond all reasonable doubt, so that he could be justly sentenced on each and every count. In this way, although no one could provide a meaningful answer to the question 'Why did this happen?' the agents of law and order established, at least, a clear outline of what had happened and so, in some sense, brought order out of chaos. Due process, or the rule of law, proved sufficiently strong and flexible to deal properly with an orgy of destruction and was not compromised.

For those at the Site in the moments after Bryant had driven away up Jetty Road, the rule of law must have appeared anything but strong. Their assumptions about their own safety and that of other law-abiding citizens had been smashed. There was nobody to protect them. The first police would not arrive until almost 3 p.m. when the first helicopter touched down. But in the meantime, as they set about doing what they could to meet the situation, people from beyond Port Arthur, bringing help of different kinds, were starting to arrive.

In Tasmania the state government provides free emergency care and transport for the sick and injured through the Tasmanian Ambulance Service (TAS), which has a fleet of eighty ambulances, known to their crews as 'trucks'. Three-quarters of these are stationed in or near the population centres and are staffed by full-time, salaried officers. The needs of country areas are met by another twenty TAS ambulances, run by volunteers, or by ambulances supplied by bodies such as local councils or the Red Cross, and supported in part by government subsidy.

On the Peninsula there are eighteen TAS volunteers and two 'trucks' which are moved about from one volunteer's home to another, according to whose turn it is to be on call. On 28 April one ambulance was at Nubeena, where Kaye Fox and Gary Alexander were on duty. This was the first 'truck' to arrive at Port Arthur. It dashed along the road linking Nubeena and the Site, arriving, reportedly, at 1.46 p.m., only a few minutes after Bryant left the service station. The other ambulance was at the home of Colin and Robyn Dell at Taranna and was directed

Lesley + Mark friends

to go first to the Fox and Hounds so that by the time the Dells reached Port Arthur a number of ambulances from Hobart had raced to the scene and further emergency crews had been flown in by helicopter.

One of the few buildings at the Site erected after the convict period and the only one still used regularly by the local community is a small weatherboard church close to the towering, roofless bulk of the convict church. On the fourth Sunday of every month a group of Anglicans gather here. Since the twenty-eighth was the fourth Sunday in April 1996, they were setting out from their homes in different parts of the Peninsula at about the time that the first shots rang out from the Broad Arrow.

Felicity and Michael Langley were running late because, as Felicity explains:

I stopped to wrap my sister, Kate's, birthday present. So we arrived about ten to fifteen minutes later than we would normally have done. We missed Bryant by about ten minutes. We were met at the Site gateway by one of the Site vehicles and Athol Bloomfield, the Utilities Officer, looking extremely shocked and distressed. And Mike stopped the car and wound down the window and said 'What's the matter, Athol?' He said 'There's been a massacre! There's been a massacre!' So, very quickly, Mike said 'Well, you stay here . . . and I'll go down'. Well, just after Mike went, there was an outburst of gunfire down the road . . . So we looked at one another, Athol and I. Athol said, 'There's a culvert there', pointing just beyond the road junction, so I gloomily got down into the gutter and had a look along the culvert and we established that we could both just squeeze ourselves in if we needed to.

At this stage in fact we were being kept quite busy with the traffic because people were coming from both ways . . . Quite a few vehicles got past Seascape. David Coombs, another member of the Anglican congregation, drove straight past . . . Bryant must have just driven into Seascape and David arrived wondering what was going on . . . We had to be quite fierce from time to time because people had plans. They wanted to go to Port Arthur . . . I wasn't saying 'There's been a massacre!' I was saying, you know, 'There's been a bad accident. I'm afraid you can't go in' . . . Most people were very good. Most people turned straight around . . . We'd been there half an hour—at least half an hour—I'd gone across to the forecourt of the service station just to check that the woman in the car was dead . . . I also went across and begged a cup of coffee from Jim Laycock's photographic place for Athol . . . then two men came over to us, very distressed, saying, 'Isn't there anything we can do to cover the body? Because Zoe Hall wasn't covered. Everyone else had a tarpaulin over them . . . Well, fortunately, we were able to find one of those shop-blanket things. We were able to put that over her . . . And then, much later Mike came and collected me and I went down and did hot, sweet teas for the SES people who were on barricades.

Another church-goer, Alan Imber, also helped direct traffic away from the toll-booth at a time when nobody knew if the gunman would return.

I got to the top of the Site between a quarter and ten to two and I could see David Coombs and Felicity Langley on the road and Athol Bloomfield . . . I was very concerned about him because he was more than busy. He must have been given the job to control any traffic at the entrance. He was the only Port Arthur official in that area at all and he had access through the fire-brigade truck with the two-way radio to Ian Kingston. They were in touch. First thing Felicity said to me was 'Get home quick.' 'Go home', she says. I said, 'Well, I'd better stay and help you.'

That's why I stayed on. There were three of us, plus Athol. There was a lot of traffic coming from Nubeena. A lot of traffic . . . Just behind us were four bodies . . . We were concentrating on the tourists. We had to stop many cars . . . We didn't tell 'em a lot. We just said there'd been an accident down the way.

> *We were concentrating on the tourists. We had to stop many cars . . . We didn't tell 'em a lot. We just said there'd been an accident down the way.*
>
> — ALAN IMBER

Steve and Pam Ireland took over the medical practice on the Peninsula because they enjoy outdoor activities such as surfing and bushwalking and, like so many others, were entranced by the beauty of the place. All this, they felt, out-weighed the disadvantages of a practice which was, as Steve Ireland has said, 'relatively isolated and a difficult job as far as the number of on-call hours you have to work'.

By 28 April 1996, the Irelands had lived near Nubeena for over four years and were an accepted part of the local community.

I was up grading my road on the tractor. Pam was down in the house. She got the call down there and then she sort of buzzed off up the road and picked me up on the tractor . . . The story at that stage was that four people had been shot at Port Arthur and as I jumped in the car—'cos she tore off like a hare—I said, 'Well, these things are usually over-reported and there's usually a lot of panic and there might be one person injured and three people running away or something'.

So anyway we sped out there in great haste and the first thing we saw when we got out there were the bodies at the toll-booth and more bodies as we went down the road . . . When we got down there, there was an incred-ible quiet and stillness to the whole scene. Obviously people were just stunned . . . 'Well', I thought, 'the first thing you have to do in this situation is decide where every-body is and . . . decide whether the area is secure.' So I said, 'Is the area secure?' And the first thing you hear is 'No. We don't know where the gunman is. We don't know whether he's coming back.' . . . This was just a totally overwhelming experience. I mean, the brain's whizzing round in your head trying to take in all this 'cos there's people just lying everywhere. There's shot people, dead people lying all over the place. So I quickly scouted round trying to get an overall picture of what was where and trying to get some help organised . . . I raced round the bus area just looking at who was there in the buses, did a quick scout round just to see the extent of it. There didn't seem to be a limited extent.

I thought, 'Just how wide is this?' . . . .Then I went into the Broad Arrow and had a look in there. The Broad Arrow looked like a set-up in a movie with all these bodies placed around. It looked quite eerie, really. Very artificial. All these bodies just placed around, some in quite unusual postures. It had a definite air of unreality to it but there were injured people there and people attending to them . . . I started to try and see who was injured plus tried to get all those injured into a central area so we could actually triage them [sort according to the urgency of their need for treatment] and organise priorities of treatment. And this was very, very difficult to do because you didn't know how far it extended. I'd seen there were people cradling dead relatives in their hands and they were severely injured themselves. It was a very difficult time trying to get the mind around the whole problem . . . Then there were tourists just milling through this whole situation. I was trying to establish a bit of order here, so I said to them, 'Clear everybody out so we can see who's injured and what we've got and then start bringing them in' . . . At that stage I think we had one ambulance down there . . . I sent someone round to start getting all the names and the injuries and trying to label people. We'd just started to bring them in, we'd started the sorting-out process when the first helicopter arrived with the Tasmanian ambulance people on it. So that made a big difference then. We were able to get a lot more organised at that stage . . . There were people there who were quite severely injured and the ambulance brought in others but by and large, the process from then on proceeded fairly smoothly until all the injured were evacuated. The evacuation went extremely quickly because the helicopter support we had was one flying in and one flying out. It was absolutely magnificent.

Meanwhile, Ian Kingston was trying to establish a form of command post in the Information Centre. He spoke to the police, impressing on them the need to find the gunman and to prevent him returning to the Site, rather than coming immediately in force to Port Arthur. He saw to it that his SES unit and some of the local volunteer fire services were called in to help with tasks like searching the bush around Jetty Road for anyone who might be lying there wounded, or taking the names and addresses of witnesses. But soon he began to have trouble ringing out.

> *The evacuation went extremely quickly because the helicopter support we had was one flying in and one flying out. It was absolutely magnificent.*
>
> — STEVE IRELAND

We had one phone in the Information Office that had its own line, its own number, an unlisted number. That was an emergency phone . . . The real problem with the switchboard was the media ringing in. That was jamming it. It wasn't so much us ringing out. Phones were just running hot. At one stage I had a phone in each hand, you know, just trying to talk to people . . . Later that afternoon I was getting phone calls from 'CNN News' in Atlanta in America asking what the situation was. They could tell me we had a hostage situation at Seascape. They wanted to know where Seascape was. I was getting more information from the media outside of Australia than I was getting from any emergency service in Tasmania . . . The Site was virtually isolated.

To make matters worse Craig Coombs, the General Manager of the Historic Site, together with the Retail Manager, Lesley Kirby, Mark's wife, and other members of the management team were attending a seminar at Swansea on the east coast. Eventually a call was put through to them and they all set out at once, driving south at high speed. Long before they arrived Mike Langley had appeared to take responsibility for any major decisions.

It was my responsibility as a Board member to go down and do whatever had to be done. If necessary to take charge or if not to take charge, to just be there and provide the level of decision-making that was needed from the Authority. So I went down to the Information Office. Ian Kingston . . . was acting effectively as incident commander as far as I was concerned . . . He had it under control so I didn't have to do that. But I made certain he knew I was there. I then went to see Wendy Scurr . . .

I think I actually met her in the car-park as I was going across to the Broad Arrow. We went in together. She had come out and was going back in again and I joined her. I asked her if there was anything I could do just as another pair of hands . . . There were two doctors who were actually visitors to the Site working in there, and there were two or three people standing round holding drips and things like that . . . There were bodies all round the place . . . There was nothing I could add to the resources that were in there at the time. So I came out and basically stayed around the Information Centre to make decisions if they were required—they weren't really—and to provide support for Ian if he needed it because in circumstances like that it's useful to have someone standing beside you, separate from you, not interfering but able to supply support if needed. It was clear it was going to be a thing of huge importance so I rang Ray Groom who's the Minister for Tourism and told him what had happened.

Having done that, it also became apparent that we were going to be overwhelmed by media in the very near future and so I rang Sue Hobbs at home—Sue at that stage was our Public Relations Officer—and asked her to come in. One of the better decisions of my life. Her husband, Brian Allison, came as well. While Sue was getting on the telephone . . . I got Brian to go and get some chairs from the store because we had this mass of people—three, four, five-hundred people—and they were getting tired because they had nowhere to sit down. So we got a small work-party with a truck to go to the store for chairs and put those out.

The crowd was also getting hungry. After handing out some packets of lollies from the Information Centre, Mike Langley realised there was a mass of confectionery in the Broad Arrow. Helped by another former army officer who had been sheltering in the Commandant's House, he brought all the lollies and biscuits he could find in the café and put them on the tray of a truck parked in front of the Information Centre.

The Wilsons also brought food and urns to make tea and coffee from the Frances Langford Tea Rooms, while the welfare section of the SES helped with the work of providing refreshments and, as time went on, local restaurants sent in food and drinks.

Mark Kirby went off to find blankets:

I think Aileen Kingston, who had come down from the tollbooth, yelled to me to grab a ute and go and find some blankets. We had people in shock and we had to warm them up so I jumped in the ute and they said 'Here, take Steve Howard with you!' Right. And they whispered in my ear, 'Liz is dead' (Steve Howard's wife). So we went off to a number of different buildings, actually broke into buildings, smashed the windows, the whole bit . . . We ended up at the pub, the Motor Inn, and they gave us great armfuls of blankets and probably about fifty or sixty towels that we took down and gave out to Wendy and the rest to try and do a bit more to help the first-aid people. And around that time I was in front of the Broad Arrow and one of the ambulance people was having trouble opening a door to the retail section and he was calling out for help. And I said to him 'I'll go get the key' . . . I walked into the Broad Arrow and right at the front door was a dead man . . . at this stage they had covered over the faces of some of the people and he had a tea-towel over his head but he had a halo of blood surrounding his head which I think was about an inch and a half on the floor . . . Paul Cooper, I found out later, had gone round and covered over people's faces, which was all they could do . . . I believe in hindsight that I went into shock when I saw that man, even though I knew Lesley was at Swansea . . . I had to then go and make sure that she wasn't in her office dead on the floor. I went through to that side of the building and in my peripheral vision I could see bodies on the ground . . . There was an Asian couple sitting at a table: the lady still had a fork in her hand, and right in front of Lesley's office was a poor lady who had been shot in the head . . . There was blood all over the walls and all up the ceiling. The door to Lesley's office was ajar and I walked straight in and I was then confronted with Jason Winter's widow, her father and her son. And Mrs Winter is on the phone speaking to relations so I closed both the doors to Lesley's office and I'm playing with the boy, keeping him occupied while she's talking to the relations . . . At one stage her son had tried to go back into the restaurant and I had to pick him up and stop him from doing that. I couldn't imagine any place worse.

Colin Dell, who had the second Peninsula ambulance parked near his house at Taranna, was cutting firewood with a chainsaw on his block. His wife, Robyn, was carrying the pager.

When the call came she signalled to Colin who turned the saw off and went to the phone.

> They said to me: 'Colin, we have a mass shooting at Port Arthur.' So I said, 'Oh yeah. When's the exercise going to be finished?' And they said, 'This is not an exercise. This is a definite situation. We have a mass shooting at Port Arthur.' . . . So we both left in ambulance number 721 a few minutes later and headed down towards Port Arthur at high speed with lights and sirens going. Once we got to the top of Blink Bonnie, which is a hill hear Port Arthur, we proceeded down and people in cars were waving to us and we didn't respond to their waves and then one car with its windscreen shot out parked itself in a position where we couldn't get through. They advised us that the person we now know as Martin Bryant was standing on the road shooting at the cars.

The car with the smashed windscreen belonged to Anne Wardle, who was travelling with her three friends. Although they had no idea of Bryant's whereabouts and realised he could very well have decided to drive after them in pursuit, they were doing their best to warn any cars travelling down the highway towards Port Arthur. The Dells turned around.

> We decided we'd better get out of there and go round the long way. At that time we were feeling very, very scared. We didn't know whether Bryant was stationary or whether he was still in a car and considering coming towards us. We were trying to get messages out on the radio

but we were in a black spot so we proceeded to go up the forestry road so that we could get high enough to be able to get messages out about what was going on but unfortunately communications were so bad in the area that we had to give up. We were going to go via a road system that would have brought us out at Taranna but about a mile along the road there was a flaming great tree across the road so we had to back out of there.

According to Robyn:

When we established radio communications we told them about the situation and that we had to go the long way round and I also asked them to . . . tell all volunteers who called in to attend if possible but to go via Nubeena . . . Although I saw the speedo touch on 140 at times we seemed to be standing still. As we were leaving Nubeena, the central radio room asked us to go to the Fox and Hounds instead of the Historic Site . . . The Nubeena ambulance was already at the Site . . . As we were driving past the shop at Port Arthur there was a small white car parked in the driveway as if it was heading out to come on to the road . . . and I said to Colin, 'There's a dead lady there'.

Colin continued:

We pulled into the Fox and Hounds and as we got out of the vehicle we could hear shots from Seascape. We could hear the boom-boom-boom—intermittent shots still being

fired . . . The shots were very definite and very scary and
at that stage we didn't know about police or anything.
Anyway we pulled up. I asked what the story was and
they said 'We've got four patients.' Sue Williams was in the
actual entrance between the two lots of doors there. She
was lying there . . . anyway I sort of dived on to her and
said 'Are you all right?' She spoke to me. I could see she
was injured but I just wanted the initial triage factor . . .
I went to Linda next and she responded . . . All four
patients were conscious, communicating and alert, which
meant we didn't have any immediate life-threatening
positions. We then had to start looking at the injuries
and deal with any bleeding control. But whoever did the
first-aid work at the Fox and Hounds did a bloody good
job. All the patients were lying down except for Simon
Williams. He was walking around, but he'd been dressed
and his arm was secured. Susan and Linda were both on
camp stretchers.

Robyn went to Linda, who had been wounded in the right arm.

It was shattered from the elbow to the wrist. She was
worried that she had lost a lot of blood. There was a fair
bit around but not too much, and her blood pressure
revealed that she was not hypovolaemic (dangerously
short of blood). I reassured her and padded and ban-
daged her arm. Attempts to put on a splint were futile.
She was in too much pain, even with Entonox, to splint
it properly, so all I did was pressure bandage . . . Suddenly
I realised there was a police officer in our midst—not

one of our local lads. He was organising evacuation of the hotel and told Colin he was there to protect us.

Presumably this was Pat Allen's partner, Perry Caulfield. In the meantime, Colin dealt with Doug Horne.

I found out what his injuries were . . . He'd already had good first-aid . . . I was starting to deal with Susan and by that time Dunalley ambulance had arrived with Jodie Branch, Roger Garr—they're both volunteers on the same basis as Robyn and I are—and, fortunately, they had a paramedic with them called Jimmy Giffard. He'd only just come off night shift, had had about three hours' sleep, and they roused him out and he joined Jodie and Roger with the Dunalley truck and they came past Seascape . . . They decided to take a punt and come that way, which they did and got away with it. We were only there four or five minutes when they arrived. We were greatly relieved to have Jim with us because he is permitted to do much more than us. He's a paramedic so he was able to start administering IVs and the other stuff that we can't do. We eventually did the preliminaries and made sure everybody was stable. Pain control was a big problem. We currently use Entonox or 'laughing gas' as it's commonly known but it's not adequate under these circumstances. Jim didn't have morphine with him in the truck . . . Then we got Simon, Doug Horne and Linda and loaded them into Dunalley's vehicle. They took those three people back through Nubeena to Hobart. And they wouldn't have wasted much time on their trip.

Robyn recalled 'They called in at the nursing home at Nubeena to get some more Entonox . . . and they proceeded on and I think they met some paramedics at Taranna who put an IV in Linda and gave her morphine.'

Colin and the others were left with Susan, the other Canadian.

Jim decided she needed helicopter transport so Robyn, Jim and I went to the Historic Site then. So we left the Fox and Hounds with the sound of guns still going off in our ears. The thing was, the people at the Fox and Hounds thought they were the only ones . . . but we could hear the Nubeena ambulance giving the information through to headquarters about how many were dead. During this whole sequence of time it sort of went from three to five to eight . . . then all of a sudden to twenty-plus. At that stage twenty-eight were known dead and the people at the Fox and Hounds, including us, were just blown away mentally. But at least we knew where he was—and the coppers were there—so we felt a bit better about things. But the people at Port Arthur still didn't have a clue where he was until we arrived and told them 'He's pinned down'.

The police were not confident of this until much later although the news that Bryant was several kilometres away and that police were gathering at Seascape would have done something to allay fears at the Site. According to Robyn:

I was driving and as I drove in through the toll-gate area Colin said, 'What's wrong with your driving, Delly? Can't you drive straight?' I couldn't answer . . . All the bodies were covered and I knew I had to dodge them. We saw a car parked in the bushes at the side where the staff who work in the toll-booth park their cars and I recognised it as being that of my cousin Aileen Kingston, and I thought, 'Oh no! Don't tell me she's been shot!' I went very slowly . . . and although the bodies on the ground were covered there were still pieces of clothing poking out and I knew I hadn't recognised any as being Port Arthur Site uniforms so I breathed a sigh of relief and continued on. Then there were three more bodies I had to drive round and they were covered so I didn't recognise them as being those of the children. I drove on down to the Site where there were other ambulances. One was our own ambulance from Nubeena and then there were town ambulances and helicopters coming and going and people milling around outside the Broad Arrow. I saw familiar faces of the salaried officers from Hobart, which was a great relief—Andrew O'Brien was one. He was the officer in charge of the situation there . . . I saw our doctors—Doctors Pam and Steve and our friend Peter Roche's fiancée, Robyn Kroger, an off-duty nurse who also helped to treat the injured. I pulled up outside the Broad Arrow.

Colin took up the story:

We heard on the radio that the café was the area for wounded people to go to for care. Anyone who was alive they brought them out on to the verandah in front of the Broad Arrow. So we went there. We needed pain relief for Susan and Dr Pam dealt with that. Beautiful. Absolutely top piece of work. Jim wasn't able to get an IV into her—a cannula—and Dr Pam administered morphine. We wanted to helicopter Susan out, but there were people in worse shape than her so we ended up road-transporting her . . . I went on to the verandah just to see if there was anything I could do and then I spotted Brigid's face. She was lying next to the wall. I went and spoke to her and she told me that she had a bad wound on her leg and was waiting for transport. And then Jimmy Giffard collared me and said, 'I think you'd better come and have a look inside the Broad Arrow . . . People are going to talk about this for years to come and if you don't know what's in there you're not going to know when they're telling you bullshit. I went with him . . . Peoples' heads were covered with tea-towels . . . I walked around . . . Three of the victims were still sitting in their chairs, in the same position as they were when they were shot. The Asian couple I remember well . . . and there was an old gentleman in the corner so he had a wall behind him and a wall to his right-hand side and he still had his cup attached to his hand . . . in exactly the same position as you'd expect a person to be having a drink except for his head slumped into the corner. I didn't go any further than that.

Robyn also decided to go into the Broad Arrow and, like some others, found the scene weirdly calm and unreal, 'like a scene out of a movie where props had been put in place'.

While some of those who entered the café feel that they still have not recovered from the horror of the scene, the Dells remain grateful to the paramedic who suggested that they face the nightmare.

> We're glad that we did that because there's nothing we weren't aware of. We didn't sort of feel that we were blacked out on anything. I think if I hadn't seen inside the Broad Arrow I'd be still wondering today what was there and I don't wonder any more. It's not real though. It's just like something I might have seen on television.

The Dells were needed to escort a bus carrying the walking wounded, relatives of the injured, and some ambulance staff as far as Taranna, but once their ambulance was on the Arthur Highway, they were able to pull away and race Susan Williams towards Hobart. Beyond Sorell, some twenty kilometres south of the city, two causeways linked by a finger of land called Midway Point, lie straight across a long, shallow arm of the sea. By then everyone had heard about the shooting. Colin recalled people in the traffic on the causeways being just magnificent.

> We had our lights going. We could actually see a man with his danger lights flicking and he was standing in front of his car and he'd stopped all the traffic and he was calling us through. We expected to be held up there but that gave us a good run through and we got a good run through Midway Point and then we had another good run on the next causeway when people realised and gave us the road.

Robyn believes that 'Their thoughtfulness helped us get through. It helped us get through physically quicker but emotionally it helped us, knowing we were not alone'.

The Royal Hobart Hospital had just formed a disaster plan. In fact, hospital staff had spent eight months reviewing their strategy for treating a major emergency and had completed the review only a short time earlier. The plan was immediately put into operation. Eight fully staffed resuscitation teams and five fully staffed operating theatres were ready before the first patients were flown in by helicopter.

This was made possible not only by good planning but also by several fortunate coincidences. On 28 April a Royal Australian College of Surgeons' course on early management of severe trauma was in progress so the hospital's directors of emergency medicine and surgery, as well as others involved in the course, were immediately available. It also happened that on that Sunday three rescue helicopters and their pilots were on hand; normally at weekends there is only one.

Their thoughtfulness helped us get through. It helped us get through physically quicker but emotionally it helped us, knowing we were not alone.

— Robyn Dell

Thirdly, a training session for volunteer ambulance officers was in progress at the headquarters of the Tasmanian Ambulance Service. One of the people attending the session was Glen Imber, the youngest son of Alan and Barbara Imber. Glen is a member of the Tasman Council, and owns and manages the Old Trading Store at Premaydena, halfway between Taranna and Nubeena.

On 28 April, there were approximately sixteen or twenty course participants. This course was held every fortnight and we had volunteers from all round the southern district . . . From Tasman there were six of us, including myself and Gary Linnell. We were the two who went to the Domain with the choppers . . . What they used to do was come round to the units but they decided to pool their resources and get us into the headquarters in Hobart. It takes about six full-day sessions—six Sundays—before you qualify. And what they do is get permanent officers and they take us through lectures. There's also training done at unit level, which doesn't have to be done by permanent officers—mainly things like getting to know your vehicle. We have a training session every month after qualifying because you lose your skills if you don't have training in progress. We actually had the Supervisor for Tasmania Ambulance lecturing us at that particular time and the door burst open and he was called out . . . He ducked his head back in and said, 'We'll have to cancel. Something's happened.'

News of the shooting came through and Glen waited in the radio room as the death toll rose. Finally he went with Gary Linnell to the Domain, a large grassy area flanking the Arthur Highway as it runs towards the city and the hospital, and, when helicopters began to arrive shortly after 3 p.m., helped transfer patients to road ambulances. All the roads had been blocked off and one-way streets had been turned around their way for the short ride to the Royal.

A photograph of Glen bending, grim-faced, beside a stretcher appeared on the cover of the *Bulletin* of 7 May and became, like the photograph of Walter Mikac holding a spray of irises at the Hobart memorial service, one of the images which defined the events of 28 April. Despite this, Glen feels that his availability in Hobart was not quite the lucky chance it might seem and that he could have been more useful at Port Arthur. At the same time, the presence of the Director of Tasmanian Ambulance, Grant Lennox, who was able to go straight to the radio room was undoubtedly an advantage.

By the time the Dells came across the bridge that spans the Derwent River and came speeding towards the hospital along the streets that had been cleared of traffic by police, they found that everything at the Royal was running like clockwork. According to Robyn:

> We backed into the ambulance parking bay and there were orderlies there to help us unload, there were triage doctors and nurses with their gowns and identification as to their station in their job—whether they were triage nurse, whether they were orderly, whether they were doctor, whether they were clerk . . . It was wonderful! . . . We were taken aside into one of the staff-rooms. The counsellor was already there. Everything was set up with hot drinks and sandwiches . . . A bit later I spoke to the doctor who had triaged Linda White and he showed me the crossed finger sign and he said 'We think her arm will be saved.' He said, 'Whatever was done there was good.' So that gave me hope for her. After we'd been consoled we went up to headquarters to refuel and restock the truck.

Colin was going to head off after replenishing the vehicle:

> But they said, 'No, no. Don't go anywhere. We want to have
> a chat to you.' Anyway, CISD, which is Critical Incident Stress
> Debriefing, is a voluntary organisation within the police,
> fire and ambulance services. The people in those jobs
> counsel each other. So we had a defuser debrief that
> night at ambulance headquarters with one of the CISD
> team. And that was excellent. That was the first debrief and
> the best one. Everybody went through the process of
> explaining what they had done and basically how they felt
> about that.

Robyn remembers going down to the tea-room and seeing
the Boss—Tasmanian Ambulance Service Director, Grant Lennox.
'Big cuddles all round.' Colin and Robyn then went on home:

> We stopped at the Devil Park at Taranna . . . Our other
> ambulance was there and we just stopped to see if every-
> thing was all right . . . The SES were manning the
> road-block. Some of the local residents were there man-
> ning the road-block. There were firemen. And the police.

The Taranna Devil Park is owned and run by the Hamilton
family, who had been startled earlier in the day by the appear-
ance of Anne Wardle and her friends with their story of a man
shooting at cars from the Seascape gateway. When the police
began to arrive, the eftpos machine was disconnected and an
old phone hooked up. John Hamilton, a former journalist,

explained later that by then, they had four phone lines, a fax and a photocopier for the police. The reception centre had become the forward command post. As night fell hundreds of police and dozens of media representatives converged.

Superintendent Barry Bennett, the officer in charge, is magnificent. His assuredness permeates through the whole of the operations centre. There is no panic, his decision-making is firm and sound. From time to time he addresses journalists and cameramen in our car-park . . . The village baker arrives with a heap of sandwiches and I busy myself making coffee for the police team but my heart is not in this task. I am glad when the Salvos turn up with a catering trailer and barbecues.

Over at the Tasman Council Chambers in Nubeena the Mayor, Neil Noye, and the Council's General Manager, Greg Burgess, had set up an operations post of their own. According to Neil:

At around 4.00 p.m., the police contacted me and requested Council plans of the Seascape cottage. We got those out and took them over to Police Headquarters at the Devil Park where I introduced myself.

I advised them we would keep the telephone lines open from the Council Chambers for anything they needed . . . We remained there that night and gave our first media interview at about 12.30 a.m. on the Monday. The media wasn't supposed to have got through because of the road-block. The interview went well but it was pretty unexpected . . . At around 2.00 a.m. the police contacted me and wanted a bulldozer supplied to Seascape to block the entrance and possibly provide protection for any subsequent police action. We made arrangements for that.

∿

Back at the Site Mark Kirby had hardly had time to draw breath. He had made sure that Brigid Cook's children were being cared for, given the keys of the safes in his wife's office to Mike Langley, helped the Wilsons set up their urns and joined the party dispatched to fetch chairs. There were still people locked up in the museum in the Asylum building and they had nothing up there.

So we took off and grabbed another tea urn and bits and pieces and went up and gave them cups of tea and whatever else in there . . . One of the ladies had asked for disposable nappies for a baby so we took off for those and came back . . . Later on I had to go and get a formula bottle for a lady. The car was in the car-park . . . This went on like that basically right through till dark.

As Mike Langley explains:

The police presence gradually built up and coming towards dusk something came through on the radio or phone to the police officer who was in charge down at the Information Centre. He made some comment about Bryant being contained at Seascape, and I asked 'When you say "contained", d'you mean you've got him in the house or is he in the grounds?' I've got a military background: unless you have him contained in the house you haven't got him contained unless you've got a ring of people who are standing shoulder to shoulder . . . About twenty minutes later word came through that they were not certain he was in the house. Then the business came of shots being heard beyond 'Clougha', the most southerly of the Civil Row houses, used at the time as staff offices, which then caused the police commander to put the word round to all the places that lights were to be put out and people were to make themselves secure—as I subsequently learned, in places like 'Clougha', people were lying on the floor. Certainly we put the light out down in the Information Centre . . . with the glass windows you felt very exposed.

Meanwhile Steve Ireland, with an ambulance and police car, was making a last sweep of the bush alongside Jetty Road in case any dead or injured were still lying concealed in the undergrowth.

That's when I discovered Walter's family and that was rather a horrific experience . . . The people who'd been shot up there, they were covered up. And then we went along the road to the Port Arthur shop and there was a girl in the car there who had been shot. And we just looked around the bushes and the local area as wide as we could to see if there was anybody else. And at that stage it was dark and a car came up the road from the direction of the Fox and Hounds. There wasn't supposed to be any cars there so we thought it might've been him coming back so we all hit the dirt pretty rapidly 'cos the police only had 38s while he supposedly had night-sights. We thought he had an infra-red sight on his rifle so you felt very vulnerable because we only had these little pistols with a stopping distance of about ten feet, if that.

So the cops and the ambos and myself we all hit the floor at that stage when we saw this car go by. To this day I still don't know who it was. And then it came over the police radio that he was out—that this fellow had escaped the cordon down at Seascape . . . so we decided we'd better bail out of there. So we went back to the Youth Hostel and there were a hell of a lot of people milling around there. A lot of police . . . Pam and a whole lot of other people weren't there and I thought they were still back down at the Site so I started to stroll back down there . . . I started to feel very vulnerable. This fellow with night-sight just wandering round! Pam apparently had been bailed up in 'Clougha' with a whole lot of other people who thought this fellow was coming back and they'd all just piled into the house. That was a period of quite dramatic traumatisation for a lot of people . . . Many people were very frightened. They had a photostat machine with a green light that was reflecting and people saying, 'Turn it out. Turn it out!' So they were trying to flick all the switches and pulled the plug out so the thing would finally turn off.

There was a lot of apprehension and terror. Someone saying on the radio 'Get us a gun down here! Or get us some armed protection!' and that sort of upped the ante on the panic levels a bit. And Walter was there as well, moaning because he'd been told by Pam that his family were dead . . . So that was rather a bad experience for a lot of people. I think everyone there was very upset by that experience . . . Eventually there was a message to bring everyone up to the Youth Hostel . . . Bryant was never out, of course, but someone had heard some gunshots out the back and the police thought there might have been a second offender and were playing it safe. So they put that message out for that reason but that really did make people feel very insecure. It was quite frightening, actually. After seeing so many dead people you thought, 'Well, who's next?'

A little earlier, Mark Kirby, too, had joined a search-party moving through the darkness. Although a few people who knew the Mikacs were aware that the bodies under tarpaulins south of the toll-booth were those of Nanette and her children, most of the staff had not realised this. Walter had arrived from the golf course long ago, and had been searching for his family. Someone suggested that they might still be hiding in one of the buildings so a group of volunteers armed only with torches and a walkie-talkie went off to comb through the ruins. Eventually they were told to abandon the search and go to 'Clougha' for a de-briefing session.

We went to 'Clougha'. Walter was in there . . . That was when Pam Ireland turned up. And when Pam turned up and came into the room I knew what was coming. I knew

Nanette was dead. It was as simple as that . . . So while this is going on, everybody turns up for this meeting and they were all trying to march into the building and I'm arguing with them about not going in when a car door slammed. I'm sure of it. I was out the back and there was a noise and a couple went off to check it out. And the next thing you know it's the gunman. He's back. And we were all forced into 'Clougha' and it was bedlam for about a quarter of an hour.

The blackout and subsequent terror created fresh difficulties for Ian Kingston. He was trying to get people who had given their names and addresses out of the car-park or the various buildings that had served as refuges, and away from the Site.

We had to get another coach down to take the people away . . . In the museum we had about a hundred people, sixty in some of the houses. We had to get them out. We sent some SES and fire guys up to get their names and addresses . . . The buses were just about to depart, the last couple, and the police rang in, 'There's been shots heard over behind the Port Arthur Motor Inn. There's going to be a blackout'. So we had to turn off all the lights. Everyone had to get inside. Hell of a mess! So there we are, in the Information Office, trying to tidy up everything and pacify visitors who were still there and co-ordinate the last of the incident and Bryant at large, as we thought.

Many friends and relatives of those who had been killed had been taken to the Farm Overseer's house, and, just before

Jeans first shop.

the blackout, had been about to move up to the motel where the police were waiting to take their statements. Once the alarm subsided they were brought across for interviews. By now, the motel was crowded. Anita Bingham had been brought there to wait for her father who soon arrived to take her home. Felicity Langley was making sandwiches in the kitchen. Brendan and scores of other police were waiting to interview witnesses.

> We were told to get their names and addresses and start organising transport for them to be brought back to the Police Academy at Rokeby, near Hobart, if they wished, where some counselling would be made available to them. We were also required to take statements from those people who were prepared to talk to us or were able to talk to us. Other senior members had duties in relation to who did what, who went where and what needed to be done.

One officer has been critical of the way in which these procedures were carried out:

> I found it intolerable that they would fly in Tactical Response Group members from Victoria to help, they would fly in pathologists and scientific people from the mainland to help, and the witnesses and other people were being herded around like cattle on the night, and then told we needed their names again. Two of the local people down there just flew me. They said 'We've already given the police our names three times in the last half-day.

How many times do we have to give it to you?' I felt embarrassed to be a policeman.

Other police insist that they did their best under very difficult circumstances and that with poor communications, hundreds of people moving around and SES volunteers, as well as police gathering names and addresses it was inevitable that some witnesses should be questioned several times. They also claim that everything possible was done to spare the feelings of the friends and families of the dead and injured, and to provide counselling as quickly as possible.

Quite early in the afternoon Ian Kingston had managed to get a message to Hobart, asking for counsellors to be sent to the Site. He was trying to organise a debriefing session for staff in the Youth Hostel just before the blackout was imposed. But the counselling team had been held up at the police forward command post at the Taranna Devil Park, so that it was quite late in the evening before any counselling was available at Port Arthur. As the night wore on, more people left for their homes. But for Brendan, the most difficult part of his involvement in the incident was just beginning.

Later in the evening—I believe it was around midnight— I was approached by a colleague. He was asked to find three people to go into the café, and asked if I was prepared to go, to which I said I would. Two other colleagues were chosen or, I would suggest, possibly volunteered to go. We walked down to the café.

There were crime scene guards supposedly keeping people away. The scientific people were inside. They

were doing their work and photographing the scene . . .
There were two or three bodies lying on the ground near
the buses in the car-park. They were covered. I remember seeing the bullet holes through the coaches. And we
were told there were twenty-odd people inside so between
the three of us . . . we'd do all of them . . . but no more
than seven each. We were required to go through the
bodies, make notes of the positions they were lying in, and
attempt to identify them.

One of my colleagues went through first and I believe
she checked the first six or seven . . . I went through
and dealt with the next seven, starting with the back left-
hand corner . . . I believe we were at the scene for
between two and a half and three hours. The number of
people coming through that café was unbelievable. I
walked outside and spoke to a colleague who was doing
road-block duties and I said to him—I knew he had two
young children—and I said to him, 'You've got no reason
to go into the café and please don't go there because
you don't need to see it.' And this guy—he's a policeman of twenty years' experience—I just hope that he
didn't go.

Unlike the Dells, Brendan feels that the problems he has
experienced since that night have been caused by what he
saw in the Broad Arrow, and that other colleagues are paying
a price for letting their curiosity get the better of them.

By now the Kirbys, the Langleys and the Irelands, after gathering along with many others in the Youth Hostel, had left the

Site. Steve and Pam Ireland went to collect their son who had been waiting at a friend's house.

The first thing we did was go straight there. Everyone just went to their children and grabbed them. Nanette and Walter's children were part of our group so if they could just die like that I s'pose anyone can die like that. It made you feel very vulnerable, very fragile. So that was the first thing every-one did—ran straight to their kids and cuddled their children for security . . . We went home and tried to go to sleep. And the air of surreal-ity was augmented by the sound of Hayden Nichols driving his bulldozer . . . I thought it was a bulldozer and I thought 'What on earth is that? Who would drive their bulldozer at night?' But that's what was happen-ing. They had asked him to take his bulldozer round to Seascape. So he did.

Everyone just went to their children and grabbed them. Nanette and Walter's children were part of our group so if they could just die like that I s'pose anyone can die like that. It made you feel very vulnerable, very fragile.

Although it seems unthinkable, the death toll at Port Arthur might easily have been higher had it not been for the swift, expert and courageous action of a number of people trained in first-aid. Some were members of the State Emergency Service.

Until I began research for this book I had no clear idea of the function or value of the SES. I did not appreciate how versatile it has become as a life-saving force in remote areas like the Tasman Peninsula or how dedicated its volunteer members are. They train, week after week, for no reward and on 28 April turned out in force to grapple with a situation that went much beyond anything for which their training had prepared them. Some, having worked all afternoon, stayed on through the night, helping to rig up lighting at the toll-booth where bodies were still lying on the road.

Another group of first-aiders whose prompt action helped to save lives were the crews of the local ambulances. Again, these were volunteers, again, all too often taken for granted: the crew of the Nubeena ambulance who arrived at the Site within minutes of the shooting; the Dunalley crew, with their off-duty paramedic, who 'took a punt' and drove past Seascape; the Dells who worked away at the Fox and Hounds with the sound of Bryant's rifle going off repeatedly in their ears as he fired at the police pinned down in the ditch across the road.

Then there were the off-duty doctors and nurses who came forward at the Site, presumably emerging from cover when they had no idea where Bryant was or when he might reappear. There were the Irelands, the local doctors who went on treating patients even when they knew the area was not secure. There were other members of the public, like the bus driver who attended to Brigid Cook, and some that I have not even mentioned, like Denis Gabbedy, the mainland police officer holidaying in Tasmania, who left the shelter of the Wilsons' bakery to cross the open space in front of the Broad Arrow because he thought his first-aid training might be of use. There are some whose names I do not know and, no doubt, still others who came forward and gave assistance without being noted by anyone whose accounts I have heard or read. And there were, of course, the members of the staff of the Historic Site of whom, again, I have named only a few. Many of these were trained in first-aid and some, like Wendy Scurr, who is one of the Peninsula's volunteer ambulance officers, were members of a local unit of one of the emergency services. Staff members went on tending the wounded when nobody knew whether the gunman would return. Ian Kingston heard that the yellow Volvo was parked near the toll-booth and, not knowing that Bryant had taken the Nixons' BMW, believed for some time that he was prowling the Site on foot. They also faced the scene in the Broad Arrow even though some, as a result, have suffered the kind of psychological damage that Brendan, the police officer, felt must follow from looking inside the café.

> *The hospital's emergency strategy has become a model for the rest of Australia, and all those involved have been widely praised.*

The medical personnel who came by ambulance or helicopter from Hobart, and the doctors, nurses and support staff gathered at the Royal Hobart Hospital gave exemplary service. The hospital's emergency strategy has become a model for the rest of Australia, and all those involved have been widely praised. 'Tasmania's health team should be very proud of the manner in which they responded to the Port Arthur tragedy', said Grant Lennox. 'Through their skilled efforts all those who were injured and not killed almost instantly at the scene, are still alive today.'

Since these survivors included Bryant himself, the hospital staff showed not only dedication and skill, but courage as well. They had to cope not simply with two bomb threats made by people who resented the care bestowed on the gunman, but also with a string of abusive phone calls and, in some cases, harassment in the city streets.

Lives were saved, too, by a host of people who put themselves in danger to warn others or help them get to safety: motorists who stopped to issue warnings; the church-goers who stood in the open road while the sound of gunfire could still be heard; visitors who assisted one another; staff who tried to get people away from the Broad Arrow or the car-parks, hurried them into cover or made sure nobody left the safety of a building until the coast appeared to be clear. Even apparently minor contributions like providing chairs or blankets or hot sweet tea—as so many did—may well have saved lives where the victims of shock were elderly and frail. And it must be remembered that much of this was done during times when the police could not be sure the gunman was contained and even when they believed he or an accomplice was at large.

It may well be true that, as one police officer has complained, some of his colleagues were at times insensitive or disorganised. It was unfortunate that people at the Site, who were already traumatised, were put through terrifying ordeals like the 'bedlam' in 'Clougha' which followed the police demand for a blackout. But given the extreme difficulties under which the police were working they, in fact, achieved a creditable result and what in hindsight might look like an over-cautious handling of the crowds forced to huddle in darkness at Port Arthur was prompted, no doubt, by a desire to save lives. Even though they doubted their own success in keeping Bryant pinned down at Seascape, he never managed to escape. Later the journalist John Hamilton praised the chiefs of the forward command post at the Devil Park: 'Bennett and Fielding and their team have done a superb job under extraordinary circumstances. No further lives have been lost. In some ways that alone is a victory.'

Lives were saved, too, by a host of people who put themselves in danger to warn others or help them get to safety.

And it was the same determination to save lives that lay behind the acts of extreme courage performed by the people who met the gunman face-to-face, behind the self-sacrifice of those who suffered serious injury or were killed in their attempts to protect someone else. As one person moved about leaving a trail of destruction, horror and death, hundreds of others responded by evincing concern for the lives and well being of individuals and by demonstrating a living social conscience under the most testing of circumstances.

In view of all this it is astonishing that several public figures have announced during radio or television interviews that heroism is dead in 1990s Australia, apparently because no-one managed to overpower Martin Bryant until he emerged from Seascape. Anyone who has taken the trouble to look closely at the evidence will see all too plainly that a number of people stood up to confront Bryant—including three or four in the Broad Arrow and Jim Pollard near the toll-booth—and were immediately shot.

At the sentencing hearing Damian Bugg had this to say:

There has been a lot of speculation since this incident as to why someone didn't take some step to either appre-hend or bring to an end Bryant's behaviour on that afternoon. But when you look at the time span of what occurred in that café . . . it's quite understandable that there was no violent physical reaction to curtail what he was doing, the time just wasn't there, the opportunity wasn't there, and there was nothing available to those people to defend themselves or take any step to stop him.

And yet they *did* attempt to stop him. Apart from the unarmed men like Anthony Nightingale, who never got beyond getting to their feet, there were all those who tried, in some cases suc-cessfully, to stop the gunman's murderous progress by pushing others to safety or by shielding them in some way from the bullets.

The courage involved in such actions may not accord with any grandiose concept of 'heroism', but until recently Australians have preferred their heroes to be low-key. The towering arche-typal figures of European myth—the lord of life and death, the warrior-prince, the knight errant, the gallant leader who sits apart brooding over his destiny—have never cut much ice in this country. The ballads in which convicts and bushrangers are erected into 'gallant heroes' have a tongue-in-cheek quality; the Man from Snowy River is upstaged by his horse, and even Ned Kelly in his armour made from plough-shares is a subversion of the European hero.

James Parker, a film-maker who lives on the Tasman Peninsula, made these comments:

> The Australian hero is a person of self-sacrifice. From the two world wars we have Simpson and his donkey and Weary Dunlop, neither of whom probably ever fired a shot in anger. The reason that these men have been selected for sainthood (and it is nothing less) is that they were not warrior-kings; rather, they were citizens willing to sacrifice themselves for the people and the communities in which they lived.

In Hollywood the debased but inflated progeny of the warrior king are alive and well, acquiring new powers as special effects grow steadily more spectacular. Superman, Xena: Warrior Princess, Rambo and Braveheart have swept in upon us, some flying through the air, some catching swirling blades in their bare hands, some spraying lead, some overcoming legions of armed aggressors with a storm of karate kicks. In a society where more and more people—especially the young—are condemned to long-term unemployment or membership of a sub-class, to a sense of alienation and powerlessness, the movie, the video and the video game in which you can identify with the invincible are enormously seductive.

These fantasies of the solitary and violent hero may have played a part in the seduction of Martin Bryant. One witness after another described the carnage he had wrought as being 'like a scene out of a movie', 'like something I've seen on television', 'like a set up in a movie'. It seems, too, that some supposedly responsible commentators have been seduced into believing Xena and Rambo represent the realities of Australia's past, and have failed to recognise the genuine heroism of the people of 28 April for what it is.

FALLOUT

~

No matter how good you are, you don't understand.

— RON NEANDER

The fallout from the Port Arthur massacre is incalculable. Damian Bugg, the Director of Public Prosecutions, spoke at the sentencing hearing of the sufferings of five groups: those who lost family members or friends; injured people; eye-witnesses; the broader community, and the people from that broader community who helped to deal with the incident. Some people belong to more than one group. Carolyn Loughton and Neville Quin, for instance, lost family members and were themselves severely injured. Most of the injured, apart from some who were shot as they drove past Seascape, witnessed the death or wounding of others. And members of the broader community, like the Irelands, who witnessed the immediate aftermath of the shooting, dealt with the injured on the day and later found themselves involved in the treatment of traumatised patients and other aspects of their community's recovery.

It is impossible to quantify the sufferings of even the more clearly defined of these groups. The broader community extends in all directions, embracing people who knew the dead or injured as colleagues, neighbours, school-mates, faces in the street; total strangers in Montreal or Manchester who wondered where, if not in Tasmania, anyone could find safety in today's world; investors from the Middle East who were, it's said, scared away from a sixteen-million-dollar tourist development at Tasmania's Lake St Clair; Peninsula families who found their sense of security shattered and their livelihood threatened yet felt guilty for worrying over their own troubles when they thought of what Walter Mikac had lost.

The plight of the bereaved was made worse by the exceptional nature of the circumstances under which their friends and relatives died. This was no accident or natural disaster, but the work of another human being who appeared to have no comprehensible motive for what he had done, and who, unlike most mass murderers, remained alive. How could anyone else fully imagine the feelings of those whose nearest and dearest had been gunned down by this person? How could anyone relieve their sense of isolation by sharing their pain? Damian Bugg put it like this:

> The grief and anguish that is experienced following the sudden and unexpected loss of a life's companion or a lover, a parent, a child or a cherished friend is a human emotion which requires no explanation, and in times of strife or human conflict or even natural disaster we tend to accept loss of life or significant personal injury as one of the exigencies of the environment or times within which we live. There is no everyday experience which can condition the human psyche for a violent assault upon it of the proportions of Martin Bryant's senseless criminal behaviour on 28 April 1996.

The suddenness of the deaths was cruel enough. Walter Mikac, speaking on 'A Current Affair' said: 'It's like in an afternoon my whole life's been erased'. The rest of us, as Damian Bugg points out, can have some understanding of the grief caused by sudden death in a war, a bushfire or a flash flood. This was different and more cruel. David Capper, whose partner, Andrew Mills, was killed in the Broad Arrow, commented: 'I could understand if it was a car accident or an earthquake, but when this happens it totally wrecks you'.

Unfortunately the difference between the Port Arthur massacre and a natural disaster and, consequently, the peculiar nature of the suffering experienced by the bereaved has not always been appreciated. A good deal of the lore cited by counsellors who were helping those who had lost friends or family members at Port Arthur and other victims of the shooting was drawn from studies of events like the Ash Wednesday bushfires at Mount Macedon in Victoria in 1983 so that the wisdom which emerged was of a rather general kind. It was recognised that chronic stress effects, anxiety, depression and family tensions make up part of the legacy of disaster—any disaster—but much less attention was given to the painful and pressing difficulties faced by those whose dead are the victims of a mass murderer, or to the still more exceptional ordeal faced by those whose dead are the victims of Martin Bryant.

The relatives and friends of those who died at Port Arthur have to contend first with rage, hatred and a desire for vengeance. It's hardly surprising that Carolyn Loughton, who lost Sarah, her fifteen-year-old daughter, and was shot in the back herself should demand the re-introduction of the death penalty and express the hope that Bryant should rot in hell. But he remains stubbornly alive, and, so far as one can tell, feels no remorse. Other mass murderers—Vitkovic in Melbourne's Queen Street, Frankum in Strathfield, Hamilton in Dunblane, Ryan in Hungerford—have taken their own lives, but Bryant survived his killing spree to loll and giggle in the dock while the relatives and friends of his victims looked on. The experience of Port Arthur has no counterpart in the aftermath of a natural disaster and no precise equivalent that I know of in the sequel to a multiple murder. It remains for most of us unimaginable.

The anxiety that comes as a response to disaster has been described as a common reaction commonly expressed by reluctance to go far from home, meet new people or try new things. The implication is that such a reaction is irrational— as it might be where the disaster is a flood, a fire or a cyclone. Yet when the disaster is a mass shooting perpetrated by a human being, the anxiety of the survivors—their fear of meeting strangers, for instance—may

It's like in an afternoon my whole life's been erased.

— WALTER MIKAC

be more rational than most of us care to believe. Already, in some cities across the world, the kind of fears experienced by a survivor of Port Arthur are treated as something more than symptoms of Post Traumatic Stress Disorder. And already there are voices of warning raised in Australia. William de Maria, a Queensland lecturer in social work, has said: Simply, humans are not designed to live in the sort of societies we've designed for ourselves. We're becoming increasingly isolated, stressed, expected to perform harder and some of us cannot keep up. Some of us snap. It's easy to say a killer is either mad or bad. But we are creating them ourselves.'

It's preferable, of course, to turn away from this kind of thing, to go on living your life as though such statements meant absolutely nothing. Those who have had someone precious to them murdered by a stranger with a gun are hardly in a position to turn away, and may very well come to believe that we are not designed to live in the societies we've designed for ourselves. If we treat such a view as nothing more than a manifestation of the stress that follows any kind of traumatic experience, then we condemn the victims to a deeper isolation—and, it could well be, condemn ourselves to a similar plight in the future. Perhaps, then, one of the most awful burdens that Bryant's victims have to bear is that of seeing the writing on a wall most of us pretend just is not there.

The bereaved of Port Arthur, unlike those who lose people they love in accidents or natural disasters, have been left to grapple with baffling, tormenting questions. Walter Mikac has courageously faced the question of why mass killings are becoming ever more common in our society and answered it in terms of the availability of military-style weapons. For this he can hardly be commended enough, but beyond that issue lie other questions about the way we live. And beyond these general questions lies the enigma of Martin Bryant. Why this young man instead of another? A great deal has been written about his various possible motives. He saw the Martins as 'very mean' because they refused to sell him a small farm that they were much attached to. He is said to have harboured grudges. The Tasman Peninsula is full of rumours about the days when his parents owned a shack near Port Arthur and Bryant, as a child and adolescent, got into various kinds of trouble with local people. He is said to have been punished for tampering with boats and to have been ordered out of the Broad Arrow by its former owner. But all this seems absurdly inadequate. None of it adds up to a comprehensible motive for killing total strangers who had done him no harm. It would be easy for those who loved them to come to feel that their deaths were without meaning and end by finding no meaning in anything. Again, we owe it to the bereaved and to ourselves, to remember that Bryant is a human being, albeit a highly unusual one, and do what we can to grasp the reasons, general and particular, for what he did.

Damian Bugg has also detailed other hardships borne by the bereaved. He spoke of 'extreme grief, in some cases requiring hospitalisation and depression which for some people extended to considering suicide', of difficulty in dealing with everyday tasks and in concentrating, of careers compromised and relationships broken. There were financial problems caused by the need to take time off work or by the loss of income from a partner, a parent, a sibling or a son or daughter.

Some of the bereaved also suffered physical injury. Most were tourists, knowing no-one beyond the people with whom they had come to Port Arthur. As Damian Bugg explained: 'People who suffered serious injury on that day were not only subjected to physical pain . . . but also the anxiety and apprehension caused by the isolation of the site at which this incident occurred. Many waited in fear of death whilst appropriate arrangements were made to evacuate them from the area.'

The most seriously wounded had to undergo emergency surgery, followed by a series of further operations. Some found themselves physically unfit to carry on with their jobs or enjoy activities which had given them pleasure. Some couldn't even drive a car any more. Some will never recover from the physical and emotional damage they sustained on 28 April; damage compounded often by loss of income and increased expense.

Linda White, interviewed on 'A Current Affair', explained that almost every aspect of her life had changed, and that the operations needed to rebuild her shattered arm had a huge effect on the rest of her body. Like the bereaved, the injured suffered from a whole host of the ills which follow trauma. Seven months after the event, Peter Crosswell admitted that it had placed an enormous strain on his marriage, that he couldn't 'handle stress very well these days', and was often irritable. Others have suffered from insomnia, nightmares, phobias, daytime flashbacks and bouts of nausea or uncontrollable weeping. Many are still suffering in some or all of these ways.

In detailing the impact of Bryant's actions on eye-witnesses, Damian Bugg pointed out that 'the realisation of how close they came themselves to suffering such violence . . . has had a shattering effect on many people'. He added that many have felt anger and bitterness, disbelief and powerlessness. Some suffer from panic attacks, social insecurity and claustrophobia in crowds or public places. Like the bereaved and the injured they may have trouble sleeping or concentrating. Colin Prout, a Canberra real estate agent who saw some of the shootings, has barely been able to work since 28 April. 'I lose it. I could take pressure before. But now if I've got three things at once I say "Stuff it, I'm going home".'

Others have developed eating disorders, lost weight, taken up smoking or started drinking too much. Some have become violent while others are terrified by any sign of violence. A great many are troubled by various forms of guilt. Angie Dalton, who spent nearly three hours huddled with her family in the museum, felt guilty for leaving the Site. Men, in particular, are tormented by guilt because they were unable to attack Bryant or stop the shooting. Some fantasise about leaping into a car and ramming the yellow Volvo as Bryant drove away from the lower car-park, though how they could have done this in the few seconds available when Bryant had two of his weapons ready beside him, is impossible to imagine. Many—again, usually men—feel guilty and inadequate simply because they are experiencing various symptoms of Post Traumatic Stress Disorder. They think they will be despised as weak if they seek help and even wish they had been physically wounded so that they could offer some clear, undeniable reason for their nightmares and insomnia, their broken relationships and damaged careers. They become increasingly anxious about their anxiety.

The Hobart psychiatrist, Dr Ian Sale, has pointed out that when George Hennard shot dead twenty-three people in Killeen, Texas in 1991, those injured suffered lower rates of psychological disorder than the eye-witnesses who escaped physical injury. Having listened to many people who were at Port Arthur on 28 April, I can understand why this should be so.

So far as the police were concerned, the eye-witnesses—people who could say that they had seen Bryant shoot one victim or another—make up a special group from which, if Bryant had come to trial, the witnesses for the prosecution would have been drawn. But when it comes to assessing the traumatic effects of the massacre, the experiences of the eye-witnesses are similar to those of some who saw only the aftermath of the shooting: the scene in the Broad Arrow, covered bodies on the road, the ruins of Seascape. Others who saw very little but spent the afternoon shut up in one of the houses, terrified that the gunman would come back and kill them, have also shown symptoms as severe as those of people who were closer to the epicentre of the tragedy.

Out in the broader community live Martin Bryant's family, whose state of mind one can hardly bear to contemplate, as well as the scores of people who have encountered him in one way or another. Some of them have been very badly affected by the massacre. One woman who had never met Bryant but had lived in the next street in New Town telephoned me to say that she had moved to the Huon Valley and changed all her locks but still couldn't sleep properly. She lived in constant fear, yet hesitated to ask for counselling because she hadn't been directly involved in the events of 28 April.

Children have suffered especially severely. Centacare counsellors have met many who are still having nightmares and are frightened of the bad man coming to get them, of guns or helicopters. In the small town of Richmond near Hobart, these fears have been expressed in young children's drawings and paintings. A five-year-old spent the day after the massacre clinging to his teachers in floods of tears. In other schools older children have tried to explain their feelings. Ashley Norris, a Grade 10 student at Hobart's Rosetta High wrote: 'Like myself many of us have not yet had to experience the loss of a loved one over the tragedy of death, and are unable to deal with what has happened.' Ben Bannister from Grade 7 at the same school ended his poem on Port Arthur like this:

You wish you could go back in time
And make sure you were never there.

Schizophrenics have also suffered untold distress. In 1994, when Bryant applied for a disability pension, he was assessed by a psychiatrist who 'raised the possibility that he might be developing an illness of a schizophrenic type'. But Bryant was never diagnosed or treated as suffering from schizophrenia, and all the psychiatrists who examined him after his arrest agreed that, although intellectually impaired and suffering from a 'personality disorder', he was not schizophrenic. Unfortunately the remark made in 1994 led to an assertion in a police media briefing that Bryant had been diagnosed as schizophrenic and this, in turn, led to a great deal of ignorant hostility towards the mentally ill. Callers taking part in a talkback session on a Hobart commercial radio station demanded that schizophrenics should be locked up or dumped on an island and left there.

Mary Blackwood, the State Program Co-ordinator of Mental Health, tried to calm the storm:

> It must be understood that the incidence of violent behaviour in people with mental illness is no higher than in the general population . . . Whatever the final finding on the mental condition of the alleged offender, the Port Arthur incident is as foreign and as tragic to the many Tasmanians who have mental illness as it is to those who have not.

Elaine Reeves was prompted to write in *Open Mind*, the journal of the Tasmanian Association for Mental Health:

> At least three suicides in New South Wales were attributed to reaction to [the police media announcement]. It was reported that one young man who killed himself had left

a note saying he had schizophrenia and rather than be capable of such a horrific act, he was taking his own life.

Later Ian Sale, the Crown's expert medical witness, attributed much of Bryant's conduct to the autism-like disorder, Asperger's Syndrome. This created less of an uproar; where schizophrenia is a much misunderstood household word, hardly anyone had heard of Asperger's Syndrome apart from actual sufferers and their families. But many parents of children with Asperger's became worried that their children would develop violent tendencies or that all sufferers would be tarred with the same brush as Martin Bryant and persecuted.

Towards the close of his submissions at the sentencing hearing, Damian Bugg referred to members of the 'broader community' who had played some part in dealing with the massacre and its effects:

> It goes without saying that the emergency services personnel, ambulance, police officers, employees at Port Arthur Historic Site, hospital employees and people directly connected with dealing with this tragedy have all been subjected to a most unusual, even for their training, experience within their work and responsibility. For those people, some have suffered sleeplessness and other understandable responses to the stress of having to maintain control and deal with this tragic event.

Paramedics Peter Stride and Warwick Allen, who arrived at Port Arthur on the first helicopter sent from Hobart, found the scenes confronting them just 'mind-blowing'. 'Had we done war service', said Peter Stride, 'perhaps we could have related to it.' Andrew O'Brien, who took over later as the ambulance co-ordinator, expressed a similar view: 'I've never seen a war scene but it fitted my idea of what a war zone would look like. There was blood everywhere, broken crockery and furniture everywhere and bodies everywhere.'

Brendan, the police officer who was one of the three sent to the Broad Arrow to try to identify the bodies and list details, expressed feelings which are very common among those directly connected with dealing with this tragedy, feelings which tend to exacerbate their sense of stress. He seems to see himself as weak or inadequate because he is haunted by 'demons'.

A problem unique to me I think is a young lass that was fifteen years old who was one of the deceased and was wearing black fingernail polish and she had the fashionable black baggy jeans with white stitching and Doc Marten boots. That sticks in my mind quite vividly and the first night back—I think it might have been the Tuesday night—after having been there, at the end of the second day, I went out for an evening meal with a friend and we were in a hotel having a few drinks and a meal and there was a group of girls at the next table and they were laughing and having a good time. And one of them at one particular stage laughed louder and longer than the rest and I looked around and she was running her hands through her hair and they had black fingernail polish. Another—a person sitting next to her—had black baggy jeans with white-coloured stitching and I just lost it a bit. It still has a bit of an effect on me when I see young girls walking round with those jeans on. I'm slowly beating it, I think . . . But that's what sort of sticks in my mind. Two-thirds of her head was missing and she was lying on her stomach.

I still have problems with some of the news reports even as recently as a week and a half ago. They had a program on firearms and the surrender of firearms and they showed shots of the memorial cross and the amateur film of peoples' reactions when they heard the shots initially and I had to leave the room.

I've been a policeman for seventeen years and I've seen lots of things and there's guys out there and girls out there hurting a lot more than me—let alone people who lived in the area and had had no exposure to all this. I certainly wouldn't want to put myself up as being any worse or more affected than anyone else, but I've got a few demons, as you might say. But I'm getting the better of them. I'm not necessarily full-on with these professional counsellors, as you want to call them, at this stage. People listened and I guess that all they have to do is listen. But I don't know—I wanted more. I wanted answers, I think. I don't know. I don't know what I wanted. I wanted more than someone just to pat me on the back and say, 'There, there, it's going to go away.' I wanted more than people to say 'Don't worry about it. This is a normal reaction to abnormal circumstances.' I wanted more for my colleagues who I perceive are more affected than they outwardly appear to accept. Whether they are or not, I don't know but they certainly appear to be affected. Very emotional. Some of them are having dreams.

Meanwhile some of the counsellors were beginning to show signs of strain themselves. It was almost as though the people who had been at Port Arthur on 28 April had contracted a plague that went on to infect their families, friends, acquaintances, counsellors and everyone else with whom they came in contact. And in Tasmania the severity of the plague was increased by at least three different factors.

The first was lack of information. Right up until 7 November, when Bryant changed his plea of 'not guilty' made on 20 September to one of 'guilty', nothing that might prejudice Bryant's right to a fair trial could be made public. Even after the change of plea, Chief Justice William Cox insisted on continued restriction of media coverage in Tasmania until after the sentencing hearing. Justice Pierre Slicer of the Tasmanian Supreme Court explained that:

> The constraint was for a wider purpose. That is, to enable the imposition of the penalty and the conclusion to the sentencing process to be seen to have been made on the basis of what was presented . . . A community exposed to two weeks of victim stories, personal reactions and understandable calls for particular retributions, for example, the death penalty, would be confused and dissatisfied with any result because it would be impossible to separate the legal material from the intuitive assimilation of a wide range of impressions. There would be an inevitable loss of trust in the whole sentencing process . . . Constraint was not about the offender. It was about us, about our society.

This is very persuasive, especially when one considers the orgy of media excess surrounding the trial of O. J. Simpson. The way in which the Tasmanian legal system contrived to meet the challenge of the Bryant case without sacrificing the integrity of its principles or its practice is one of the more heartening aspects of the whole affair. And so is the great sensitivity and care for the feelings of witnesses shown by Damian Bugg. At the same time, the proper and necessary restrictions on the flow of information to the media and the public in Tasmania left some victims of stress feeling mystified, bewildered and increasingly anxious.

> *The way in which the Tasmanian legal system contrived to meet the challenge of the Bryant case without sacrificing the integrity of its principles or its practice is one of the more heartening aspects of the whole affair.*

Second, Bryant's various court appearances, the prospect of the trial all through October, and the November sentencing hearing all represented obstacles which the victims had to face in their struggle towards finding peace. This was true for victims everywhere, but the proceedings took place in Tasmania, dominating Hobart for days on end.

Ann Hillman, a member of the Port Arthur Historic Site staff, who was in the Information Office when Bryant started shooting, wrote in an open letter in October: 'What will happen next? What about the trial . . . How will we cope with it? All of us suffer in our own way. No-one can feel like we do, yet we're all suffering together.'

And then there are the financial costs, which have been felt to some extent by businesses, families and individuals in other countries and other parts of Australia as well as in Tasmania.

People from all over the world and all over the country, together with national and state governments, have made contributions to the Victims' Appeal Fund, the Tasmanian public purse, recently established bodies like the Tasman Trust or special collections for particular groups and individuals, but the burden on Australia's smallest state in terms of lost income and massive expenditure remains immensely heavy.

The Tasmanian economy was in poor shape before the massacre so there has been some argument over the extent to which the shooting can be blamed for a continuing decline. Between May and August 1996, business confidence in the state dropped by 14 per cent, but since the Small Business Index shows a similar drop for the whole of Australia, the Port Arthur incident might have had less influence on Tasmania's financial woes than some pundits claim. Even so, there is no doubt that the number of tourists crossing Bass Strait fell away dramatically in the weeks after 28 April. Port Arthur itself was not operating commercially in the three weeks up to 20 May and since a visit to the Site is a key feature in most package tours the effects of this mourning period were felt by tourist operators throughout the state. Things have improved since then, but it's still too early to say whether tourist numbers have returned to a healthy level. So far the evidence suggests that visitors are coming back to the Historic Site, but that fewer people are choosing to spend an extended holiday in Tasmania.

The bill facing the state—the cost of the government response—is expected to run into the tens of millions. And if Tasmania fails to recover its image as a quiet, beautiful and safe haven the money will become increasingly difficult to find. Not only the tourism industry will suffer. The Premier, Tony

Rundle, has pointed out that educational institutions which rely on attracting overseas students to provide part of their funding are also facing a problem 'to the extent that we say to parents of foreign students that they should send their children to Tasmania to study because it is a safe place'.

Unhappily, the state's reputation for safety had already suffered some damage before 28 April. In March 1993 a young German tourist, Nancy Grunwaldt, vanished while cycling down the East Coast. Neither she nor her bicycle have ever been found. Two and a half years later, in October 1995, an Italian visitor, Victoria Cafasso, was stabbed to death on Beaumaris Beach, near the point at which Nancy Grunwaldt was last seen. This mystery remains one of eight Tasmanian murders, committed in the past sixty-five years, which remain unsolved. After Bryant's arrest the rumour that he was responsible for the deaths of both young women flew in all directions. It was said—rightly, as it turned out—that he had stabbed David Martin with a knife as well as shooting him. If David Martin, then why not Victoria Cafasso? Why not Nancy Grunwaldt? But the speculation came to nothing, and Tasmania remains, in the popular imagination, both the site of the worst modern massacre by a lone gunman in peace-time and home to an East Coast murderer who is still at large.

All of us suffer in our own way. No-one can feel like we do, yet we're all suffering together.

— ANN HILLMAN

For the time being tourists, it seems, take a quick look at the eerie little island and hurry home, just as they might peer into the dark cell at Port Arthur and come quickly out into the daylight, telling themselves that the barbarity of the past has nothing to do with them. Nowadays some also peer curiously at the guides who, as Michael Langley wrote in a tribute to the Historic Site staff, still act as 'custodians of history' although 'since the 28th . . . they have become part of that history'. They, too, can be left behind.

One way of coping with the growing insecurity of the times is to see present-day Tasmania, with its murder witness guides, its city and Peninsula where a mass murderer grew up, its grisly mysteries, as a place to be rejected and quickly left, just as our forebears turned their backs on earlier violence, on another bleak past which, whether they liked it or not, was still part of their heritage, part of what they were.

True to form, the Tasman Peninsula is home to a cross-section of the different groups of people who became victims of Martin Bryant's murderous onslaught, while at the same time offering some extreme examples of the damage he inflicted. The municipality has its bereaved, including, until recently, Walter Mikac. It has only one resident who was physically wounded by a bullet but dozens whose health have been affected by the tragedy. It has its eye-witnesses and its groups directly connected with dealing with the tragedy on the day, as well as people like Elaine Ball, the community health sister, who have been dealing with it ever since. And beyond those most directly involved are all the others, linked in this small community by ties of blood or friendship or familiarity to more than one—sometimes all—the seven dead and many of the severely traumatised.

P eter Adams describes himself as an 'an artisan in wood', although he is generally regarded as a sculptor. He concentrates on making benches, which are both functional pieces of furniture and 'little icons of the natural world that we can bring into an urban setting to remind us what is beyond the four walls of our house'. Like his benches, he is big, spare and solid in a way that suggests a power to open up a new appreciation of life and the earth around us. He grew up in Michigan but has travelled widely. In 1995, while visiting Europe, he was invited to mount an exhibition of his work in several cities including the Latvian capital, Riga. He is also one of a group of artists appointed to consider designs for a memorial at Port Arthur.

Coincidentally he came to the Peninsula after suffering the same misfortune as Marlene Burton, and lives in the same area near Roaring Beach.

After returning from six months abroad, my house burned down on 21 February 1991. And that created an opportunity to look at what I was doing with my life. No longer did I have a place full of memories, responsibilities, mortgages. There was a clean slate. I mean, absolutely everything was lost. So then I decided it might be fortuitous to find a new place to live. I knew I needed to stay in Tasmania because I've lived in a lot of places in the world, and for me, this is the only place on a year-round basis that I felt there was enough excitement and opportunity. And a place where I might be able to effect a small change. You see, being an island the parameters are known. I lived in Alaska for seven years. That's physically, stunningly beautiful. Easy to make money, but then it was too extreme. You know, the weather here is never cold, never hot. Easily survived.

I left University with a history degree. Taught English for a year in Korea, then worked on a farm in Korea for a year, which got me interested in construction and carpentry. I went to Alaska . . . where I did that. Then I wanted to move more into the arts, so I studied at the University of Wisconsin . . . focusing on function. So furniture—but I never saw furniture as just function. To me it was form . . . Well, today it goes beyond form even. It goes towards what we live with. How can that tell us something about our own individual lives and the greater lives around us? Effect a healing for the world? That to me is real important.

After having lost friends through suicide, through AIDS, through cocaine overdose, it just seemed to me our world was highly troubled. I saw the Tasman Peninsula as a place where, in a simple way, I could do some good just by planting trees. So the land I bought was basically barren.

It had a few copses but out of the 100 acres, approximately 60 acres was former grazing pasture for sheep. Marginal. Really marginal, being next to the water. So over the last four years, I've put in 1240 trees. That's a small reflection on how we can live our daily lives to do good, despite knowing the odds against the world. I plant a tree but 20 million get cut down. But we all live in hope, so we keep planting the trees, despite the evidence.

I'm learning to listen so I've chosen to live without electricity, without a TV, without a radio, without a stereo. Just during this period, to learn to listen, so that I can reclaim that part that Western culture has cut off, and hopefully, I'll hear the stories again, of the trees, of the forests, of the water, of the shells, that I might in my own way tell those stories . . . You just have to be willing to listen to the story behind the stone or the wood that you're touching. And you can, through your imagination, link up with something. To me, imagination's not fantasy. It's almost genetic. It's like what Thoreau said. He says the dream of wilderness is tied into the bog in our brain. It's there, this bog. It's in us even though we might pretend that it's not, and look to cities, you know, for everything. It is within us still. So I'm trying to reconnect with that and to facilitate. That is what I'm working on. My work involves that facilitation for people, so when they buy it, they're buying something more than just a pretty piece of wood to sit on. They're buying a chance to maybe reconnect.

You have to read the story more than once. You just sit with it and meditate on it and with it and eventually it gets told to you over many readings and many sittings. So it's that sensuous aspect too, of the hand and the butt making contact with that remnant of a forest or that remnant of a mountain. In the micro is the macro—that sort of story. And it's solid. As solid as I can possibly bring into a home. It's not a thin veneer of wood or a shaving of stone. That's why I use solid timbers.

Just for that bit of soul that resides in the wood . . . And also we shouldn't fear the stories that are being told to us . . . That's why for me the Port Arthur memorial—we can't set up a memorial that's just pablum, that's sweet, so everyone's going to say, 'Isn't this lovely? Their deaths were all right, et cetera, et cetera'. We have to have a memorial that says the deaths were horrific and we have to feel that horror each time we go there to honour their memory. We can then experience that horror but also as part of the memorial there is a sense of renewal. We move from that sense of horror to the sense of renewal. We would come away moved. Twice moved. But to feel the beauty we have to feel the pain and not be afraid of going into that.

All Australia—and beyond—has had to come to terms in some way with Martin Bryant, if only by trying to forget him or by dismissing him as a freak, a 'unique person' so different from ourselves that he is hardly a person at all. On the Peninsula Bryant and the plethora of feelings he evokes—outrage, fear, insecurity, bewilderment, guilt—are hard to escape. It is not simply that the sizeable section of the population who still work at the Site have to pass the toll-booth every day, and, unless they stay in the new administration buildings to the right of Jetty Road, go down to the car-parks and the partially demolished café. Nearly everyone has to drive past the ruins of Seascape at some point to watch a football match or collect a load of firewood. Rotary meets at the Fox and Hounds. The Devil Park at Taranna is now remembered as the place that was once a forward command post. Nubeena is where the Mikac family lived.

In the school hall at Nubeena on Friday, 26 April 1996, an audience, made up mostly of elderly long-term residents, gathered to watch a collection of short films showing the Peninsula in earlier days. People laughed and nudged each other as they recognised themselves picking apples in the 1950s. Walter Mikac came in rather late with a charming little girl whom I had not seen before. In the intervals between films she amused herself by walking up the steps on one side of the stage, crossing behind the curtain at the back and popping out on the other side. She had satiny dark hair, smooth skin and bright eyes so that she reminded me of one of my favourite paintings, Leonardo's *Lady with an Ermine*, in which a dark-haired girl is holding a small supple animal—two beautiful young creatures, quick, graceful, full of eager life. This was Alannah who, forty hours later, was shot dead behind a tree. And I can never go into that hall again without thinking of her and remembering how we sat there, unsuspecting.

Places all over the district can seem infected not only by horror and grief but by the knowledge that Bryant knew them too. As well as spending a good deal of time at his parents' shack near Port Arthur he has said that he practised shooting on the Forestier Peninsula near Murdunna. In the 4 July interview with Inspectors Warren and Paine which was recorded on video and shown at the sentencing hearing, he spoke about going surfing at Roaring Beach and buying coffee at 'a little shop near the school' in Nubeena. In the past he had turned up at Neil Noye's farm asking to buy cattle, and had hired horses from Elizabeth Howard's father. At one stage he owned a small property at Copping, a village on the Arthur Highway, and went up to Sorell for some of his shopping, like most of the Peninsula's population. So while the whole country—and other countries—ask how is it that our society can produce a Martin Bryant, in Tasmania the question is more insistent, the bewilderment or frustration or guilt more oppressive.

And there is the dreadful feeling that, since Bryant knew the Peninsula so well, he might have turned up this road or that on 28 April, called at some other guesthouse, started shooting in the café at Nubeena, the 'little shop near the school', turned his gun on cars at Taranna or Eaglehawk Neck. Alan Imber wonders what would have happened if Bryant had arrived at the Site after the Anglican congregation had begun their service. What if he had heard hymn-singing coming from the weatherboard church? Mark Kirby's mother went out to buy bread a few minutes before Bryant began shooting from the gates of Seascape. She lives between Port Arthur and Taranna. Each has a general store and sometimes she goes to one, sometimes to the other. On 28 April she turned right and went to Taranna. These stories are everywhere. Bryant is in prison 'for the term of his natural life' but the Peninsula no longer feels like the safe haven that it was. As Steve Ireland

said, 'If they could just die like that, I s'pose anyone can die like that. It made you feel very vulnerable, very fragile.'

That feeling is taking a long time to dissipate. It can be made a positive force, and prompt us to value life more highly, to sympathise more keenly with people who live in the midst of violence, to do more to understand and rectify our own social ills, but for the time being, for most Peninsula residents who have suffered psychological damage from the massacre, it remains a source of great distress. And this is only one of a whole medley of emotions, many of them common in numbers of Bryant's victims everywhere, which people on the Peninsula are trying to cope with. Often these feelings are so complicated and contradictory that they become a source of anxiety in themselves.

Elaine Ball, who has kept a diary of events since the massacre, writes of being 'overwhelmed with incomprehensible feelings' during the first three months. Nearly everyone affected complains of being unable to sleep. 'I don't think I slept at all for about three days in the first week', said Mark Kirby. 'Finally you'd be completely whacked and you'd sleep right through the night and you'd get up and couldn't go to sleep the next night. Just go in and lay on the bed and lay there and look at the ceiling.'

Like many others, he found it very difficult to concentrate or get any work done. In the first two weeks:

Basically I'd get up in the morning and I would prioritise things that I wanted to do. And I would go off and I'd be ecstatic if I got one of half a dozen things done. One was to go and pick up the truck, so I did that and that was about all I did in a day. It was an effort to do anything at all.

Elaine Ball wrote of similar experiences in her diary:

Long nights, sleep won't come at any price . . . Unable to function normally for any length of time. Loss of memory, forgetting friends' names, doing strange things . . . We are in shock, we do not feel able to make these *blessed decisions* . . . Past traumas well up in individuals, becoming one.

Steve Ireland had personal experience of this last symptom. He was driving up to Hobart one day:

It might have been for the church service at St David's Cathedral . . . thinking of all the fatal and serious accidents I'd attended on the road and they were quite vivid. I mean I don't know how many times I've driven up the road and not thought about them, but every time I went by a place where I'd attended an accident it was vividly recalled. This was quite astounding: I've been driving on that road many, many times and it would never have crossed my mind. But that was everybody else's experience as well—or most other peoples' experiences. If there were any previous serious life events they were definitely revisited and rehashed.

He also found that when he went back to work after a short break, 'my concentration was just totally gone. We were absolutely paranoid that we were going to make mistakes so you had to work twice as hard at doing things.'

All this, in turn, led to other problems. Elaine Ball talks about the way in which relationships broke down because people had 'no energy for normal friendships' and how her preoccupation with the massacre, together with her increased workload, led her to forget about her own sister's death, which then made her feel deeply guilty. Anita Bingham, driving home from a counselling session and 'not thinking properly', rolled the car that she had saved up to buy.

Yet, quite soon after 28 April, a good many people on the Peninsula felt that they had more or less recovered from the effects of the incident. The Board of the Port Arthur Historic Site Management Authority met on 30 April and made its decision on the three-week 'mourning period' during which the Site would remain open but wouldn't operate commercially. Staff who wanted to return to work—provided they could find something to do—could come back as soon as they liked, but anyone who felt like taking a break until 20 May could stay at home or take a holiday. Those who needed longer to recover would be able to apply for workers' compensation payments after 20 May, which meant that if their claim was accepted, they could take six weeks off work on full pay and, if necessary, a further period on 95 and then 90 per cent of their normal weekly wage or average weekly earnings. Ian Kingston chose to return to work at once:

> The mistake I made was that I went back to work straight-away and I thought that this was never going to get me. I worked until the end of August and then I went down

in a screaming heap basically . . . I think everyone who had been working there since 28 April was at the end of their tether by then.

Within four weeks of the Site reopening, management was saying 'Everyone's getting over it'. But that was the point where the adrenalin had run out and people were getting into quite nasty situations. They were getting aggressive . . . I talked to management but I couldn't convince anyone there was a problem. People kept saying, 'They're all right, they're all right'. But I knew they weren't . . . The girls who were working in the caravan that was put there to provide refreshments until a temporary café was built at the western end of the Broad Arrow were upset and they'd be out crying behind the van . . . People who make the decisions . . . unless they're there working with them they don't know how it's affecting individual staff members.

Out in the wider community around Port Arthur, Steve Ireland and Elaine Ball found that many people, after an apparently rapid recovery, developed problems months later. Steve found things 'as bad as they've been' in November after the sentencing hearing. At about the same time Elaine noted that trauma counselling was in great demand and the community 'in chaos'. This delayed reaction or reappearance of difficulties which seemed to have been overcome is, apparently, very common after disasters of all kinds, though not everyone on the Peninsula is convinced that it is useful to be warned that you are likely to feel much worse in a few months time than you do already.

The daughter of a member of the Historic Site staff, who wants to be known only as 'Naomi', said:

They're always saying communities recover best when the recovery's 'community driven' but then they want to write the script for us. They take our stories away and give us theirs. We're all supposed to fit into these socio-logical boxes, our disaster's supposed to be like all the others. I'm not saying most of the counsellors aren't good and I know they've helped a lot, but some of them and some of the people who come and speak at meetings down here don't really see us as absolutely unique. It's OK to notice trends and ten-dencies like this backlash and be on guard for it. It's probably quite a common thing, but they can't say it has to happen here or to you or me. It might happen here or it might not. It might happen to you and not me. It's our lives, and our story, and our recovery. Not theirs. If they try to take over they just make everything worse.

> *It's our lives, and our story, and our recovery. Not theirs. If they try to take over they just make everything worse.*
>
> — 'NAOMI'

The idea that well-meant and generous advice or assistance can sometimes actually retard recovery or create fresh out-breaks of trouble has been raised in other ways by other people. Many have pointed out to me rather tersely that what is done to or for the Peninsula, what is offered from outside makes news, while what it has tried to do for itself has not attracted much attention. Sometimes when they needed encouragement the people of Tasman have been left feeling passive, humiliatingly feeble and unappreciated.

In November 1996 a great uproar arose over 'a cricket spectacular' to be staged at Port Arthur, featuring the Australian team and 'national celebrities' including Olympic gold-medal swimmer, Kieren Perkins. The aim was 'to put something positive into the area after the terrible events of April 28', to promote the return of tourists to Port Arthur, and to raise funds to help victims of the shooting. Unhappily, on 13 November the *Mercury* carried the headline 'Port Arthur Snubs Stars' and went on to explain that the Tasman Council had rejected the sporting stars' offer. This was quite untrue since the Council was all for the match. Difficulties had been raised by the Board of the Port Arthur Historic Site Management Authority, as was made clear next day. These were resolved eventually, the match went ahead and turned out to be a great success. Eddie Halton, who runs the Nubeena general store with Pam, his wife, was very appreciative of the way in which the players had donated their time 'when these guys are on really incredible schedules'— but nobody said anything about the work done by the local Events Committee, of which he is a member.

The population of the Tasman were left to reflect that even in nearby Hobart people failed to understand that Port Arthur is not the whole Peninsula, the Board is not the Council, and that, even though the whole area might be 'economically and socially depressed,' a good many residents were doing more than sit about waiting for assistance.

John McGuinness is called 'Guinea' by nearly everyone he knows. He is small, wiry, dark and surprisingly strong. After growing up in Hobart he worked for fifteen years in a car firm 'in the spare parts game' but, in 1988, gave up his job to move to the Peninsula with his wife and their young son, Adam. They came because they wanted to buy their own house, but couldn't quite afford city prices and because, at the time, there seemed to be plenty of jobs in Peninsula tourist ventures, on farms or fishing boats, and in the few remaining orchards. Things began well but within two years the marriage had broken up.

Adam stayed with his father, paying visits to his mother who lives near Hobart. Guinea settled down to life on a supporting parent's pension supplemented by income from occasional odd jobs, though, as he explains, work is harder to find now that nearly all the orchards have been ripped out and things like hay-baling have become more mechanised. Sometimes friends turn up to give him a hand and he, in turn, helps out by fixing a car or doing some fencing. At home he cooks, cleans, washes clothes, grows vegetables and keeps bantam hens. He takes his turn in the school canteen with other parents (mostly mothers) and belongs to the local volunteer fire service which nearly every summer is called out to battle bushfires. He has made up his mind to stay on the Peninsula.

Adam is eleven years old now and we've been together for six years . . . One thing that draws me about here is there are so many beaches nearby. Magnificent coastline. It's unreal seeing that from a boat down round Tasman Island and all round there. There are beaches with huge sand dunes. Also, where else can you really go where you can be on the beach and five minutes later you can be in the middle of a rainforest? A lot of people think the Peninsula is just Port Arthur whereas there's a lot more down here to see and there's magnificent views up on top of the hills. You can look over virtually the entire Norfolk Bay and it just looks great. And there's other things you see down here you wouldn't see up in town like the migration of mutton birds out in Norfolk Bay. Now when you see thousands of those round there it's absolutely magnificent. I went up Fire Tower Road the other day and 2 metres above the ground there was a hawk just hovering in the wind right next to the road. Yeah, you don't sort of see that. And the birdlife down here—all the different sounds of birds. And the quiet. That's another top thing . . . it's so quiet.

With the people round here, a lot of them I find you only have to ask and they help. Say if someone goes out fishing and they drop in, generally you can get a feed of fish off 'em. And there's always parties going on. There's generally a party going on somewhere at least once a month where they have bush dances, trophy nights.

There's things for young kids to do—you know, they have the netball. They've just started soccer. There's

tennis, basketball, touch football . . . You can generally find someone's going past your place and they'll
always give you a lift.

My neighbour Kate came over and told me her sister,
Liz Howard, had been shot. She asked if I could look after
her two young ones while she went up and saw her
parents. So I looked after her kids for that day and the
rest of the week on and off.

The funeral for Liz Howard and Nicole Burgess was
held in Koonya Church. There was cars everywhere.
There was a great mass of people there. A hell of a lot.
They even had a little bit of a bus shuttle for people
who had to park so far away. I thought that was good
. . . I had my tears then. And driving past now you
always see flowers there. There's always a great mass
of flowers there.

This reflection was depressing for even the most courageous
or robust. And by now, as Ian Kingston had observed, the
adrenalin had run out. Alan Andrews, who, with his wife Annie,
moved into Brigid Cook's house to look after her family while
she was in hospital, had this to say about the days after the
massacre:

People were protective and they were so open. It was
wonderful to see. And then, as all the considerations
came in, sometimes a sense of isolation would follow. You
see, in some ways I think one of the most difficult

things—I don't know whether it's even been talked about—is that for a while all of us lived at such heightened awareness. We were so receptive and I think since then there has been a desire to live on that edge again and life very rarely throws up those moments. Having experienced that, one is so alive that there is a desire somewhere, even if it's unconscious, to live on that edge again of such meaning, of such fulfilment. And to recognise that such awareness grew out of one of the most awful situations is very difficult to deal with. That is what I observed, and that in itself was almost a shock to me . . . I observed it in myself. And I realised that I was not the only one who felt so alive after something so awful.

The loss of energy, accompanied by a kind of nostalgia for the intensity of the early response and guilt at such a feeling, was only one of the difficulties which, as time went on, started to plague different groups in the Tasman community. Many of those who had been at the Site on the day were confronting a whole battery of problems which went beyond a sense of depression and isolation. Mark Kirby and Anita Bingham, as well as a number of others who worked at the Site but were not directly employed by the Authority, were faced with confusing issues regarding their entitlement to workers' compensation and access to counselling and rehabilitation services provided by the Authority's insurers. In the normal way the visits to solicitors or union officials, the need to concentrate on explanations and make decisions might have been handled quite easily but nobody and nothing was normal any more.

Those who worked at the Site, especially those who had been present during the first two hours after the shooting and had done so much to hold the fort until help came from beyond Port Arthur, were under extreme pressure. They had lost three colleagues. Sue Burgess, Nicole Burgess's mother and Elizabeth Howard's cousin, worked there with her two sisters and Elizabeth's husband, Steve. Some of Nicole and Elizabeth's relatives have given up their jobs, some have even left the district, but to go back to work on 29 April, 20 May or some later point meant being confronted by grief and absence. It also meant being viewed by visitors to the Site—as Michael Langley has pointed out—as part of the history of the place and facing questions about what you had seen and done on the day.

Immediately after the massacre, the Board did what it could to protect staff from the barrage of questions being fired by journalists from all over the world. Michael Langley explains that: 'We said that we really didn't want staff to talk to the media for their own protection.' But on 1 May the Board decided to hold a media conference because:

what we were feeling was that everybody else was getting talked about and this was a huge problem and has remained a problem. Everybody was getting acknowledgement. The police were getting acknowledgement. The ambulance people were getting acknowledgement and yet for an hour and a half—or whatever the time was—the safety and welfare of survivors, indeed the survival of some of the survivors depended entirely upon the actions that the staff took at the time of the incident, during the incident and after the incident. And this wasn't recognised. It wasn't picked up. That's not criticising anybody. The last thing I'd criticise is the Bishop. The Bishop gave an extraordinarily good sermon at the 1 May memorial service in Hobart. He quite properly thanked all those people, but the staff were not included. Now that wasn't his intention at all but it was indicative of a pattern that kept going on, and forever after we were trying to recover ground because the staff felt they'd been left out . . . We lost the initiative and everything we did after was trying to catch up. From the point of view of lessons learnt, the question of acknowledgment has to be amongst the highest priorities of people who are faced with managing a crisis like this . . . The people to whom the media reports—unless these people are told who should be acknowledged, they don't know.

So the objection to staff consorting with journalists was withdrawn. But after a time it was found that 'staff were getting stretched by too many requests for interviews. It was just becoming too stressful'. Again the Board stepped in and Michael Langley took over the job of media representative. At the same time some staff wanted their stories recorded, so the Board decided to commission a historian to gather accounts and write Port Arthur's own version of 28 April. Then, two days after the historian had started work, the police insisted that the project should be stopped because there was a risk of contaminating evidence which might have to be given in court. All this led a Salvation Army Colonel, Don Woodland, to report in December that: 'In the case of some Historic Site staff and their families, the cocoon of protection that was put into place from day one has been allowed to develop into a cocoon of isolation . . . The effect has been most disturbing.'

Something else that arose in part from good intentions but which ended by making readjustment harder than it might have been for the Site staff was the extent of the rapid changes at Port Arthur. Those who went back to work found that jobs were being reshuffled. There had always been a fairly brisk turnover of personnel at the Site and some who left after the massacre would have gone anyway, but now, with three staff members dead, others feeling unable to return to work and still others wanting to change the kind of work they had been doing—conducting ghost tours, for instance—the shifting from pillar to post became almost frenetic. No-one really knew who they would be working with. One employee said:

I used to get on really well with the others before but when I went back most of them were new. It was really hard because you needed support just to keep going. You needed to be with people who understood what you'd been through because they'd been through it themselves. It was like a club before—you know, we all got on—but I couldn't relate to this new lot. And then just as you were getting used to someone they'd get shifted off to do something else and you'd have to start all over again.

Marlene Burton, who had been working part-time in the Broad Arrow, feels that in the general confusion, the catering staff were overlooked altogether:

It was really strange for us café workers because they actually forgot all about us. We felt we were completely abandoned because there was nothing for us to do before the arrival of the temporary caravan. I mean, there was no work for some of the others as well but workers were allowed to go back on-site if they felt like it. A lot of workers did, but there was no work for the café workers. And we were just all feeling completely useless and at a loose end.

At the time of the massacre the Management Authority had been poised on the brink of a massive building program. Administrative staff were to be moved from Civil Row to new premises and a new visitors' centre set up behind the old Information Office. This, too, was unsettling for anyone who was already feeling insecure, especially since all these changes were accompanied by a new emphasis on interpretation of the Site and plans to improve the 'overall skill levels and professionalism of the staff . . . through education programs'. Some new members of the management team had been appointed to implement these aims.

Even in good times all of this would have led to controversy. Some people felt that conservation of the existing buildings was being neglected in favour of 'gimmicks' or that, having become a 'government business enterprise', the Authority was so busy chasing the tourist dollar that it had forgotten why people came to Port Arthur in the first place. Inevitably there were mutterings among the rank and file. Given the history of the relationship between the community and the Board, the need which many felt to vent the anger aroused by the massacre on someone or something, and the way in which anxiety can be exacerbated by change, the Authority was doomed to attract more than its usual share of hostility.

A furious row broke out over the Broad Arrow building, which some wanted left standing as a place of mourning and some wanted razed to the ground. Another row flared over the allocation of seats at the sentencing hearing. The General Manager, Craig Coombs, complained that between the staff, the community and the Board he was damned if he did and damned if he didn't.

Other quarrels began to erupt all across the Site and in the community beyond. People were accused of 'milking the system' by trying to claim money or benefits like free holidays when 'they weren't even there on The Day' or 'lived right out at Salt Water River and had nothing to do with it.' Several marriages broke down, although, as Naomi said, 'You can't blame everything on the shooting. Some of that might've happened anyway. It's just if things weren't good it made them worse.' Sadly, disasters often have this effect, so that even Dunblane is now plagued by a crop of disputes.

One group for whom things very rapidly became worse were the professional carers. Elaine Ball and her assistant were already hard worked before 28 April.

Some of our services included co-ordinating and delivering nursing care for people at home and for those returning from hospital. We also maintain the frail aged and those with disabilities within their own homes. We thought we led a pretty busy life . . . No-one could have envisaged the frantic days that followed. With all of us in our community in shock, we were suddenly inundated with numerous services all wanting to be directed in day-to-day activities . . . The health centre had to be reorganised to accommodate the new services. This, of course, meant more decisions, with workmen everywhere.

There were workshops run by trauma experts and nightly meetings, which left the staff with no quiet time to recover at the end of the day. Soon Elaine was suffering from panic attacks and mental exhaustion. Rebecca Bushby, a social worker, masseur and Faldenkrois practitioner, who represented Centacare in the emergency team of health professionals based at Nubeena, was advised to take stress leave at the end of 1996. 'It is crucial', she says, 'that Disaster Management personnel, as a matter of policy, offer to their workers what their workers offer to victims.'

> *You needed to be with people who understood what you'd been through because they'd been through it themselves.*
>
> — PORT ARTHUR SITE EMPLOYEE

Steve Ireland is also angry at the poor co-ordination of all the services and facilities:

I think the really, really important issue of this whole process is . . . there's no overall control, which should be exercised by the state but isn't, which has led to horrendous problems. As medical practitioners we've probably seen more of the affected people than anybody else and had more exposure, plus the personal exposure to the events on the day of the massacre and losing friends as well. Everybody that's had anywhere near the involvement that we've had is going to run into trouble sooner or later. I mean, everybody has and we're no exception. And we've been incredibly under-supported purely because we run a private practice, and so because we're not under the auspices of the state government directly, they've neglected us. Compare us to what's gone on in Dunblane, for instance, where there's a six-doctor practice. They instantly sent in extra doctors. They sent in a full-time psychologist . . . to give the doctors support. They organised straightaway all this after-hours relief. They didn't have to do any after-hours on-call work at all—because the content of the consultations is so distressing, facing after-hours calls is something that's really, really difficult to do. And they poured money into the place as well. And yet it was a much larger practice in a much larger place . . . The other example is Port Arthur, where the insurers brought in counsellors from a private organisation . . . being, once again, private, they were initially neglected, left out of the whole equation even though some of the most severely affected were actually over there . . . I mean we made strenuous efforts to bring them into the fold, into the recovery team and that eventually has happened but there's still this overall diversity between the private and the public which still exists and creates problems today . . .

Everybody's been sitting back waiting for us to crack . . . I've virtually reached a point where I've had to switch off for survival. So I've switched off on pretty well everything. It was obviously too much and personally, we reached a huge crisis. And I find at this stage that I'm not able to stay down here, certainly not on a full-time basis. I have to be looking to get out of the place at least part of the time.

Steve Ireland has now left the Peninsula, part of an exodus that includes Walter Mikac. The loss of population is damaging not only because particular people will be missed, but also because, if the number of residents falls below a certain level, all kinds of facilities will be lost. If enrolments at the Tasman District School, for instance, shrink much more, then staff will be withdrawn, funding axed and amenities restricted. This may, in turn, lead to more parents of school-age children moving away in search of better educational opportunities; the speed of the downward spiral will only increase.

Bill Blackwood, who settled on the Peninsula in 1987, became interested in 'all the potentials' of the area, but saw also that it was facing difficulties common in rural communities throughout the Western world: the decline of agriculture in the face of the 'get big or get out' syndrome; conflict over the use of resources; wealth draining out of the area; high unemployment; young people drifting away; declining services. Bill investigated the disappearance of the Peninsula's dairy herds and most of its apple and pear orchards in a Master of Environmental Studies thesis and concluded that, like many other rural communities, Tasman was facing a choice: 'continuing decline or the community could basically come together, look at its problems and develop some kind of common vision . . . that helps people to control their future'. With the help of his friend, Neville Curtis, a former journalist and public servant with a history of anti-apartheid activity in South Africa, and the support of Neil Noye, Bill established Peninsula Action for Community Enterprise (PACE) in late 1992 to develop a communal vision, promote small businesses and create employment. Opinions vary over the degree to which PACE has been directly responsible for the ensuing changes which have taken place in the last three or four years, but the rate of change in Tasman has certainly quickened. Tourism has become increasingly important; more small businesses like Glen Imber's store at Premaydena have opened up; and, while the drift of young people to the city goes on, the stream of retirees, alternative lifestylers and artists flowing in from the outside world has remained strong enough to counteract the exodus. At least until last April.

At the moment the number leaving in the wake of the massacre seems to have outstripped the number of new arrivals. Small businesses suffered badly during the three weeks Port Arthur was not operating commercially and some have had trouble recovering. Unemployment is up to 18 per cent. Simmering quarrels between those who want development at any price and those who are fiercely opposed to wood-chipping or quarrying or subdivision have flared up again. On paper, at least, things look very bad indeed. The Australian Taxation Office statistics for the 1994–95 financial year showed the average income for residents in the Port Arthur area as the lowest in Tasmania, which in turn has the lowest top end incomes in Australia. And the prediction is that the figures for the Port Arthur region are likely to have sunk further given the negative economic impact of the massacre.

There are a number of families on the Peninsula whose lives are severely impoverished. They have never really adjusted to the decline in traditional farming or, to a lesser extent, fishing. In the past they would have worked on the orchards, dairy farms or cray boats and would have expected their children to follow suit. Some resent tourists, 'greenies', 'blow-ins', 'hippies' and officials who push them around. Demoralised by unemployment, they often develop drinking problems, slip into violence and become vulnerable to ill health. Their young are frustrated, sometimes disruptive, sometimes despairing. Before the massacre, they were plagued by many of the problems which the shooting has created for other people, and in some cases their situation has gone now from bad to worse.

Yet in some ways the figures relating to incomes on the Peninsula are quite misleading. A number of residents have deliberately chosen to accept a lower financial return than they might have enjoyed in Hobart, Sydney, New York or Capetown because they believe that the quality of life they can enjoy in Tasman is better than anything they have experienced before. The sculptor Peter Adams lives in a converted bus with no electricity and, like everyone else in the district, no connection to a mains water supply. It would be easy to represent him as living in third-world poverty, but anyone who visited his property above Storm Bay when he opened his exhibition of beautifully crafted benches could see that he has good reason to regard his way of life as privileged and enriching.

Bob Walter, a former New York psychologist, and his partner, Penny Whistler, are Zen Buddhists who live, as far as possible, off the land, spin the wool of their goats to make their clothes, and even fashion shoes from the skins of animals killed on the roads. Although others may not live as cheaply as Bob and Penny, they manage well on low incomes by growing vegetables, keeping chickens, helping each other out, like John McGuinness and his friends, catching fish and making their own entertainment. The beaches, the clean air and water, the scenery and the bush-walking are all free—and, despite the events of 28 April, remain so.

Between these two very different groups are some who manage, by one means or another, to earn a bit—even a good bit—more: innovative farmers and fishermen like Neil Noye, who has kept his farm going by starting a contractor's business and turning to new crops such as French truffles; energetic small business operators like Glen Imber; Maree Heron, who manages to combine offering a house-cleaning service with running a pig farm; Peter Rigozzi, a self-taught builder and cabinet-maker.

All of them have been affected by the massacre in one way or another. Most are aware that, as Bill Blackwood pointed out, the Tasman community has for some time been confronted with a choice: disruption, powerlessness and decline, or unity, control of its own destiny and a new future. The events of 28 April have made the alternative sharper and more urgent. And while, for the time being, they have tipped the scales towards decline, it could well be that the struggle to redress the balance will, in the end, carry the community through into a time of new strength and very much brighter promise.

RECOVERY

~

Gracious God, Light of the World,
We ask that your love may shine for those who
have died so tragically at Port Arthur.
Lead them from the darkness of death to the light
of eternal life.
As you make the day to follow the night, help all of
us to look in hope for the dawning of a new day,
Where pain and sorrow are being healed and
confidence restored.
We ask this for Jesus' sake.
Amen.

— PHILLIP NEWELL

In the week that began with the burning of Seascape and the arrest of a man who ran in flames from the building, the long slow healing started with communal mourning, with rituals that drew communities together and gave shape to their grief, with exhortations to move on through the encompassing darkness towards light and hope.

On Tuesday vigils were held at which thirty-five candles, one for each of the dead, burned through the night. The Tasmanian Premier and leading clergy appealed to all Australians to pause at 10.30 a.m. on Wednesday for a minute's silence to remember those who had died and pray for the recovery of the injured. Across the nation flags were flown at half-mast. Prime Minster John Howard and the Leader of the Opposition, Kim Beazley, flew together to Tasmania to attend an ecumenical service at St David's Cathedral in Hobart. A section of roadway outside the Cathedral was sealed off so that 800 additional seats could be set up. A crowd of thousands assembled and the service, conducted by the Anglican Bishop of Tasmania, Phillip Newell, was relayed to television viewers around the world.

This service was important because it brought individuals together: people were able to see their own experience as part of a larger whole and find release in a grief shared by others who had faced the same demands and suffered the same kind of strain. Colin Dell went to the Cathedral with Robyn, his wife, that

Wednesday: 'Once again, still very numb. But cry? Just couldn't stop crying. Cried for days. Tears coming out and you'd break into almighty sobbing.' Robyn thinks that 'If we weren't able to cry like we have we would have ended with emotional breakdowns, I'm sure. You need that pressure relief, the ability to cry.'

Colin recalls that 'It was wonderful at the church in town. The hundreds and hundreds of people who were there. And we were in our uniforms, and all the permanent ambulance officers and all the volunteers were there.'

As Robyn describes:

We were in a convoy. We walked from Ambulance Headquarters in Melville Street down Argyle, up Collins Street. We got to the Cathedral and we were assembled to go in. And when we came out we were all together again. We had to get ourselves together down at the corner and members of the public came and patted us on the back and said 'thanks'. It was just such a wonderful lot of people. I was thinking, 'Why are they thanking us? We only brought one patient up. We didn't stop the man who caused it all' . . . Then we went in our group again with the Director and the paramedics and the rest of our volunteers.

Philip Hilton, the Port Arthur Site Education Officer, was strengthened by the service in a different way:

I was going to leave my job that night immediately after the shooting. But you always feel that way. The knee-jerk reaction, you know, saying that you couldn't cope. But you learn to cope and I found that the service at St David's Cathedral was the thing that turned me around. I wasn't going to sit around and wallow in it. That's it. I was just going to go back to work because, you know, the Bishop said we don't even imagine how we can go on. I thought 'Well we've got to . . . I'll go back to work. We'll make the transcription of convict records for the new database the focus because we won't have anything else to do. There won't be any visitors while the Site's closed and Susan Hood and I have this work.' So we planted ourselves into this.

> *The work was the therapy. We wrote to all the historical and genealogical societies that we had been in correspondence with to say 'We go on. We go on with our work. Don't stop writing to us'.*
>
> — PHILIP HILTON

As in hundreds of other instances the determination of one or two people to move forward soon became part of a broader movement, touching off new developments. Philip Hilton continues:

We came back to work within the week. The work was the therapy. We wrote to all the historical and genealogical societies that we had been in correspondence with to say 'We go on. We go on with our work. Don't stop writing to us'. And I wrote the same to the schools, 'It goes on. I know how you feel now. I felt the same'.

There were reactions. The Director General of Education wrote to all the schools and said that they had a responsibility not to ignore Port Arthur . . . not to shy away from it. And later the Catholic Education Office did exactly the same thing.

Numbers for school parties visiting the Site in 1996 were not high, but not as low as everyone expected. And soon, according to Philip, the numbers will rise.

I've spoken to a few teachers who haven't been down here for a few years and they're going to bring their school groups down next year . . . The focus needs to be put back in front of the kids. They have perceptions about Port Arthur that need to be addressed. We need to address them. Their teachers need to address them. You have to put the significance, the real significance back in front of them and . . . help them accept what happened.

Other services and rituals were taking place across the country and across the world, but, for the people of the Peninsula, one of the most important ceremonies was the memorial service held in the shell of the convict church at Port Arthur on Friday, 3 May. Just as the citizens of Carnarvon lived their lives and raised their hopes in the relics of earlier misery, so for years the people of Tasman have assembled in the ruined church every Christmas for a candle-lit carol service. The silhouette of the church is used now as the logo of the Port Arthur Historic Site but it also stands for a reconciliation of past and present, and the suffering and hope which is the legacy of the community who live beyond the Site's boundaries.

The choice of the church as the venue for the memorial service was one of those symbolic gestures which must have seemed entirely natural at the time. Amongst other things, it offered people a chance to confront the massacre scene if they felt a need to do so. Some, like the Dells, had already returned to the Site as a way of doing what Colin called 'chasing the spooks away'. Philip Hilton not only works at Port Arthur but also lives during the week at a house called 'Lithend' near the dockyard area. Most people, however, whether or not they had been present on the day, or were employed at the Site, or had suffered some personal loss were able to decide for themselves. Many chose to return at the time of the memorial service when they would have neighbours and friends to support them and ritual to act as a conduit for their grief.

The ceremony was particularly moving. At one stage children from the Tasman District School went one by one up the steps of a temporary platform under the west window, each offering a red rose to the mayor, Neil Noye, as the clergyman conducting the service read out the names of the dead. The roses were laid on a low table that might have been an altar or a coffin and glowed against the pale cloth like great drops of blood. A local girl with a fine voice sang 'Amazing Grace' and from the rocky eminence above the Site, known as Scorpion Rock, a piper played.

After the service the congregation moved down to the Broad Arrow, now banked with flowers, and wandered over the lawns, weeping, embracing, exorcising demons. No journalists were allowed to attend, and the place had been closed to tourists so that briefly, in the wake of a manifestation of late twentieth-century violence, Port Arthur was restored to the people of Tasman as it had been after the more protracted violence of an earlier time. Kate Sainsbury, President of the Tasman Peninsula Historical Society, was one of many who had dreaded returning to the Site, but after going with her niece to visit the place where Nanette Mikac had died, she felt that she had begun to come terms with what had happened.

Over two weeks later there was another much larger gathering at Port Arthur. The committee set up to organise the service announced that one of its aims was to help the residents prepare for a return to normal life on the Peninsula and that 'the format for the service, being organised by Pastor Glenn Cumbers . . . with the support of the Tasmanian Council of Churches and community representatives, will be simple, with "hope" as one of its basic messages'. This time the Governor and the Premier attended, and thousands watched as thirty-five white doves were released from the foot of a wooden cross built by Mick McMillan from Roaring Beach.

The Rosny Children's choir from Hobart sang hymns. 'They realise the significance of their role', said their director, Jennifer Filby, 'and are praying that by singing they will be able to bring hope and healing to the community.'

Still later there were cleansing ceremonies at the Site for members of the Hindu, Buddhist and Muslim communities. Symbolic offerings were made as some 700 people joined in prayers, chanting and periods of meditation. Imam Ali Eli-Senossi El-Daleh explained that: 'As Muslims, it is desirable for such a ceremony to take place so that future visitors, especially those with high sensitivities, will not be disturbed or harmed.' The Buddhist monk, Bhante Vijitgha, said that, 'If the departed know this ceremony is for them, they can be happy that the living have not neglected them or forgotten them.'

And then there were the funerals as the bodies of the victims were released to their relatives and carried back to their homes. Nanette Mikac and her children were returned to Victoria. The Martin family faced a grim ordeal, and were forced to postpone the cremation of their parents because investigators needed to take DNA samples from the bodies. So it was the families of Nicole Burgess and Elizabeth Howard, both members of the Campbell clan, who became the focus of mourning on the Peninsula.

Decades ago when the farmers and fishermen of Tasman had no metalled road to Hobart and relied on steamers for their links with the outside world, neighbours habitually offered each other help. Farm diaries from the 1890s through to the 1940s and 1950s record the sharing of tools and labour, gifts given and received, and above all, a ritualistic drawing together in times of trouble. This ethic survives in parts of the Peninsula but, in the days after the shooting, it seemed that it had revived throughout the district, stronger than ever. A neighbour who visited Don and Nancy Campbell, Elizabeth's parents, at their Koonya farm on 30 April said that she had shrunk from going to the house but, once there, was made to feel at ease. Everyone knew their role. Mourners were welcomed at the door. Gifts of food were placed in the kitchen. Although she felt she had done little enough for the bereaved parents, the neighbour emerged comforted.

It was the same at the funeral in Koonya. The church in this green village is very small, its inner walls lined with Baltic pine, its roof topped by a wooden bell tower made by Peter Rigozzi who lives next door. On the day of the funeral the church was surrounded by a sea of people. It was here that John McGuinness shed his tears along with hundreds of others. But as well as providing an outlet for grief, the funeral gave the mourners a chance to give, to find relief for their frustration in a return to the generosity expected by an earlier generation. Jo Kang-Scheit built up a successful business in Hong Kong before she and her German husband discovered the Peninsula and settled here three years ago. The funeral at Koonya astonished her:

Since I move here I try to be involved in all these social groups. To see more people, to know more people. So first I joined the Red Cross and then the CWA . . . The CWA have to prepare for after the funeral . . . Prepare the place . . . prepare the tea, coffee and put the beautiful candles and flowers and all this kind of thing . . . At this time you find out how people really are and they are doing what they can do and do their best for everybody . . . The people really care about our community. All the ladies come and they make food—cake or some sandwiches or something. Everybody bring some. And the CWA ladies have to collect all the flowers and put in the hall. I prepare two or three bunches. But everybody suddenly bring flowers to the hall. On every window, every door, beside the wall—food or flowers. And the food is on big round tables. How many tables there? Almost ten, I think, of food. At the beginning I little bit worry. How can we prepare if few hundred people come? And suddenly comes so many, many people. They said 3000. I don't know. We just think we prepare so many tea-cup, coffee-cup and we just collect back and wash again. I never wash such a lot of cups in my life. We ladies in the kitchen, you know, so busy. So, gentlemen just stand behind me and help. Everybody just bring the tea-towels and help to clean up. People really help each other and care for each other . . . Normally you just smile to the people and say 'hello' . . . but this time you find people really from the bottom of the heart . . . and everybody get together. I say to Peter 'We live in the right place'.

> *If the departed know this ceremony is for them, they can be happy that the living have not neglected them or forgotten them.*
>
> — Bhante Vijitgha

If the funeral at Koonya served as a focus for the grief of the people of Tasman, the Melbourne funeral of Nanette Mikac and her daughters served as a focus for the grief of the whole nation. Everyone felt that the stalking and killing of six-year-old Alannah when she tried to hide behind a tree was the most abominable of all of Martin Bryant's crimes. Her father, deprived of his wife and both his children in a single stroke, was seen as the most heart-rending of all the surviving victims of the out-rage. Walter Mikac, pale, bereft, but always dignified, always impeccably dressed, was much interviewed, photographed and quoted in the days following the massacre. By the time of his family's funeral on 9 May he was a national figure.

K eith Moulton is Nanette Mikac's father. Despite the loss of his daughter and grandchildren he has decided to stay on the Peninsula and gives some indication of the reasons for his choice in a piece that he wrote for the August issue of *Port Arthur Update*:

In those first weeks, the brain was 'muffled', but in due time, we realised that life goes on. There were the usual tasks to be undertaken, people to be contacted and faced, but gradually a whole new way of life began to form in front of us.

Many things we thought were important before the 28th seemed to lose a certain status and new values, new objectives, new friends, and thank God, new hope, started to become evident in our lives.

The vacancies at the dinner table were being filled with new faces. We smiled at people in our neighbourhood we didn't even know before. We appreciated the loving contact of our friends more, and gradually began to be able to meet people with our heads held high—we had not let that traumatic event permanently defeat us.

We were some of the ones that quietly sobbed in the privacy of our homes, that had faced an unwanted experience, passed through harrowing times, but with a strength that comes from outside ourselves, were once again reaching upwards to resume our rightful place in life.

My family remembers often the three members we lost, with our eyes filled with tears and very heavy hearts, and then we would recall some humorous occasions in their lives and soon that feeling of sorrow subsided to surprisingly give an added degree of strength and we were ready to cope with the next time our minds turned to the absent members of our family.

Have we all, the relations and friends of the victims, changed in the past three months? I would expect many of us to say 'Yes' to that question and as I sit here to review this past period, I have to say I am not the person I was before the 28th.

A new life rises from the ashes of dashed hopes, of lost opportunities and memories of missing family members, but I believe if we can nurture this new life, we will be the better and stronger for having been through the experience of Port Arthur on the 28th of April 1996.

The country's mood was volatile. In Hobart there had been threats against the medical staff who had treated Bryant's burns, even bomb threats against the hospital where he was held despite the fact that his fellow patients included many of those injured in the shooting. So, if Walter Mikac had chosen to call for vengeance or for the restoration of the death penalty for murder, he might well have unleashed a fury that would have been difficult to contain. As it was he displayed a degree of forbearance towards his family's killer that left those who heard or read his message amazed and abashed: 'Remember', he said, 'that the power of love and creation will always triumph over the power of destruction and revenge.'

~

Pastor Allan Anderson, who conducted the Mikac funeral service, called for changes in Australia's gun laws so that life might be more effectively protected. The tide of public opinion was already with him. One of the features of the massacre that tormented everyone was the lack of any straightforward explanation for what had happened. And in the absence of that explanation, it seemed there was no release for the need to be doing something to prevent such a tragedy ever occurring again. But if Bryant's acts remained incomprehensible, at

> *Do not let your anger be wasted on revenge. Rather let it grow into such a power of love that nothing will weaken your resolve to rid our nation of these terrible weapons of destruction.*
>
> — PASTOR ALLAN ANDERSON

least it was clear that he could not have created such mayhem without guns. So, Pastor Anderson's words reverberated around the nation and Walter Mikac became the face, the embodied justification of a campaign that the gun-lobby never had any real hope of withstanding.

For years there had been complaints about the confused and fragmentary nature of gun control in Australia. The Federal government took responsibility for restrictions on the type of gun which could be imported into the country but each state had its own laws—or lack of them—regarding such matters as licences, registration and the prohibition of military-style weapons. Because, in some states, these laws were particularly lax it was easy enough to weave one's way past any attempt at more stringent control. For example, while the Federal Government had banned the importation of weapons such as the AR15 used in the Broad Arrow, any Australian could telephone a Brisbane firm of gun-makers and order a custom-made model. A Hobart journalist who tried this two days after the massacre was simply asked to send along a licence number with his deposit. In Tasmania, Martin Bryant, who had never held a licence, had managed, by some means, to amass an arsenal of at least five semi-automatic weapons.

The National Coalition for Gun Control and their various supporters had fought a long, slow battle to put an end to the ease of access to firearms. Immediately after the massacre, they found that they had acquired some unexpected allies. The Tasmanian Parliament's most vociferous opponent of restrictions on gun ownership, Liberal member for Bass in the House of Assembly, Tony Benneworth, changed his stance overnight, urged all shooters to hand in their semi-automatic rifles and expressed support for uniform national gun laws. Other Liberals, hitherto reluctant to have any truck with what was perceived as a leftist cause, put away their distaste for bureaucratic regulation and followed suit. The Premier, Tony Rundle, announced that his minority government would act at once to ban military-style weapons and to set up a register of guns of all types. He was warmly supported by the Leader of the Opposition and by the Greens' leader, Christine Milne, who joined him in signing a tripartite agreement.

This accord was startling enough, but events at the Federal level proved even more remarkable. In the lead-up to the recent general election before winning victory for the Liberal Party, John Howard had evaded questions on gun control by insisting that this was a matter for state governments. Since taking office he had shown himself evasive on other issues, so when, on the day after the massacre, John Howard announced that he would push the states to enact tough new legislation to achieve uniform gun control across the country, there was general surprise and some scepticism.

The gun lobby was caught off-balance. Its more rabid members reached automatically for their familiar rhetoric about communist plots to leave Australia defenceless, but even those who habitually cheered them on had some trouble seeing the most conservative Prime Minister since Robert Menzies as a Red mole. In the late 1980s when Bob Hawke, Barrie Unsworth and John Cain had attempted to bring about a national consensus on gun control, the gun lobby's threats to bring down the governments that opposed them had inflicted real damage, but now such threats were meaningless since all parties—except the Shooters' Party—opted to support John Howard's stand. Even the Nationals, led by a rather hang-dog Tim Fischer, rallied—apart from a few mavericks—under the Howard banner.

The Prime Minister pressed on relentlessly in a way that brought reluctant admiration from even his most virulent opponents. He called an urgent meeting of state police ministers, took the chair, and hung on until he had achieved an agreement very close to what he sought. A week earlier Queensland, South Australia and the Northern Territory had all seemed likely to make trouble over the banning of semi-automatic weapons, but on 10 May, having won a concession regarding the use of low powered semi-automatics by farmers, their police ministers fell into line.

It was, as John Howard claimed, an historic agreement, that marked an enormous shift in Australian culture towards the possession, use and ownership of guns. The meeting had agreed to restrict the use and possession of automatic and semi-automatic weapons to police, members of the armed forces, professional shooters and, in the case of low-powered semi-automatic .22 rifles, farmers with special needs; institute an effective, nation-wide gun register; observe minimum licence requirements, such as genuine reasons for the ownership, use or possession of a firearm and compulsory safety training for all licence holders; and enforce strict safety standards for the security and storage of all guns. There were other provisions, too, relating to the recording and control of sales, including mail-order sales between states, and to a nation-wide buy-back scheme designed to compensate the owners of surrendered weapons and funded by a national Medicare levy.

This wasn't, of course, the end of the matter. There was a long period of dispute, with some quite moderate gun owners complaining that things had been taken too far, a fracas over crimping, and confusion over concessions to Queensland farmers. But by the end of 1996 Howard had largely achieved his objective. Gun controls had been tightened in all states and already 250,000 prohibited weapons had been handed in. None of this, as the Prime Minister pointed out, guarantees that tragedies will not recur in the future, but the controls, together with a new public awareness of the danger posed by military-style weapons, have done something to make them less likely. As the editor of the *Weekend Australian* remarked:

The slaying of thirty-five people at one of the country's most historically significant sites will haunt the Australian psyche for a long time. The lives of those who have lost friends and relatives have been changed irrevocably. The knowledge that their loved ones' deaths have . . . led to . . . reforms that should make Australia safer, might shed a little light on to these, their darkest days.

In the concerted push for more stringent gun control another kind of light, another kind of hope, shone out briefly. The spectacle of political parties setting aside their differences, finding common ground and working together to produce an effective result was, to say the least, thought-provoking. In Tasmania Christine Milne, leader of the Greens, saw the tripartite agreement between herself and the Labor and Liberal leaders as a model of what might come about if those elected to Parliament were to abandon the party warfare inherent in the Westminster system and devote themselves to pooling ideas and working out solutions together. Such a vision seems unlikely to become reality but, since Tasmania's minority government is proving more stable than expected, the idea that the Port Arthur tragedy might have brought about an increased measure of cooperation between political parties in matters other than gun control is not quite as wildly idealistic as one might have thought before the shooting occurred.

Meanwhile, nobody had time for theories of government on the Monday after 28 April. There were huge numbers of practical tasks to be accomplished. Many of these were organised by highly professional and dedicated people without whom some of the victims would not have survived and many would have suffered even more than they did. A number of these people were members of the Peninsula community, which is not as passive or as demoralised as the image imposed on it by some carers or experts and most media reports. The initiative and courage displayed by the people of Tasman themselves in struggling towards their own recovery deserves to be far more widely known. At the same time, the community owes a great debt to a wide range of outside agencies.

The part played by the Royal Hobart Hospital in counteracting the destruction wrought at Port Arthur can hardly be praised enough. The newly revised major emergency plan which came into operation that Sunday afternoon has become a model of its kind. Its great virtue is its flexibility, which makes it adaptable to a whole range of different disasters and, on Monday 29 April, enabled it to go on working in the face of one of the most extraordinary set of circumstances any hospital is likely to encounter. Eighteen injured patients had been admitted, some requiring repeated surgery partly because gunshot wounds are treated by 'debriding' or the regular clearing away of dead tissue as the injury heals. Late in the morning, Martin Bryant, whose legs, bottom and back had been severely burned, was brought in by ambulance, so that the hospital had to contend with a flood of police followed soon after by threats from vengeance-seekers and still tighter security arrangements. And then there were the bodies of the dead to be accommodated, wards turned into morgues and preparations made for post-mortems. All this, while journalists from all over the world prowled the hospital precincts, and a stream of victims' friends and relatives, many of whom had never been to Tasmania before, came shocked and bewildered from the airport.

Gary Knight from the Royal's Public Relations Office is proud of the fact that the principal architect of the colour-coded emergency plan, with its seven branches, is a locally trained Tasmanian, Rod Franks: 'Dr Franks and Dr Smart, the Director of Emergency Medicine—he trained here too—are always being asked to go and give lectures about it. All over Australia.'

According to Dr David Smart:

> *We smiled at people in our neighbourhood we didn't even know before. We appreciated the loving contact of our friends more, and gradually began to be able to meet people with our heads held high—we had not let that traumatic event permanently defeat us.*
>
> — Keith Moulton

The emergency staff coped very well partly because of prior planning. We had plans ready to meet a situation which had the potential to overwhelm us. Also, the very fact that we were not found wanting enhanced the recovery process.

Since 28 April we've gone forward fairly positively although like everyone else we've had our ups and downs. Those who were most heavily involved in the incident are obviously affected by reminders, but the knowledge that we were able to cope with such a traumatic and taxing situation is helping us to move forward.

Studies of the psychological effects of mass murders make it clear that those who are able to talk about their experiences

soon after the event are less likely to suffer severe or protracted traumatic reactions. With this in mind, Critical Incident
Stress Debriefing teams went quickly into action on 28 April so
that the Dells and other ambulance officers went through a
'defusing' session on Sunday evening. The police were in a
difficult situation. While the ambulance officers were coming
with their patients into Hobart, where the Critical Incident
teams were standing ready, the police were streaming out of
the city in their hundreds. Almost inevitably there was a delay
in the debriefing of some officers, including one of Brendan's
colleagues, who arrived back in Hobart to find that his wife
had received counselling because she was married to a policeman who had been at Port Arthur while he was still waiting to
be 'defused'.

Over twenty non-government organisations provided counsellors. In Hobart, Centacare's Rebecca Bushby initiated and ran
'Rest, Revive, Survive', a free, month-long program of mas-
sage for all those whose work had involved them in the tragedy.
Salvation Army and Church leaders in other states prepared
to send in groups of experienced disaster-response workers. The
military offered counsellors who had served in Vietnam or
Rwanda to assist in briefing and debriefing counselling teams,
and the state Education Department was quick to organise its
own program in schools. The Director of Education visited
the Tasman District High School and, according to one of the
teachers, offered help on the school's own terms instead of
telling the staff and students what they needed. They asked
for—and got—a security guard. By this time, Bryant was ringed
by police in his hospital bed, and there was no danger of
attack, but the sight of their own guard at the school gate did

more than anything to allay the children's fears. The guard was also useful in keeping journalists at bay so that the school's counselling sessions went on without interruption.

The principal responsibility for the provision of counselling services belonged to the Department of Community and Health. On Sunday afternoon as soon as news of the massacre came through, officers of the department started fielding offers of help, mustering their forces and deploying them to five different centres. The first of these was at the Rokeby Police Academy, across the bridge from central Hobart, not far from the Arthur Highway. Here a Port Arthur Incident Recovery Centre was set up to receive some of the more severely affected visitors from the Site. Other counsellors were stationed at two Hobart hotels, which had offered to supply free accommodation to visitors brought from Port Arthur by bus, and at Hobart airport, where friends and relatives of the dead and injured would soon be arriving. The fifth centre was at Nubeena on the Tasman Peninsula.

Each centre could be reached by a hotline but also provided face-to-face counselling sessions for anyone who needed them. By Friday the centres at the hotels and airport were no longer required, but the Incident Recovery Centre, transferred across the Derwent to central Hobart, went on providing an around-the-clock service with three phone lines, each staffed by counsellors working four-hour shifts. On the Peninsula a team of thirty-five counsellors offered a 24-hour service from the State Emergency Service headquarters opposite the police station.

By 1 May, only two and a half days after the shooting, 300 people had received help from one of the centres. Over the months to come the two remaining centres supplied almost 3000 different counselling or information services to five times that number, coping with cases of delayed reaction and supporting people through the difficult period leading up to the sentencing hearing.

By late November things had quietened down but Alex Shouten, manager of the Hobart Incident Recovery Centre, explained that between 150 and 200 people were still seeking help—some from private practitioners—and about six extra staff were still providing services in the Tasman area. The recovery program, funded to the tune of $1 million by the State and Federal Governments, was likely to continue for at least a further twelve months. A Community Recovery Co-ordinator has been appointed to work with the Tasman Council and its Recovery Working Party and a full-time social worker/counsellor allocated to the Nubeena Health Centre.

As well as supplying counselling services, the Department of Community and Health has done a good deal to try to relay information to the community. Leaflets on signs of stress and trauma have been sent to every household in the state, explaining that help is readily available, and have been circulated to all Tasmanian GPs, suggesting ways in which the massacre is likely to affect the emotional and psychological well-being of anyone involved. In July the Port Arthur Incident Recovery Centre began to produce a leaflet called *Port Arthur Update*, which has been made available to everyone connected with the shooting. It contains advice on subjects like helping children cope with trauma, information on how to apply for assistance from the Port Arthur Appeal Fund or the conduct of the proceedings against Martin Bryant, and articles or letters by people such as

Nanette Mikac's courageous father, Keith Moulton, whose letter has been reproduced earlier in this chapter. Few people would doubt the value of the various counselling services. Anita Bingham, for one, says that 'since this happened seeing counsellors has helped me that much . . . I couldn't have done without it.'

~

The Port Arthur Incident Recovery Centre in Hobart also worked closely with Damian Bugg, the Director of Public Prosecutions, whose handling of the Bryant case and of the people directly affected by the shootings deserves to be studied by prosecutors everywhere. Already, long before 28 April, he had developed a special interest in victims' issues and had reached conclusions which were now to be put to a quite extraordinary test.

Since the 1960s there has been increasing interest across the world in the rights of victims who have suffered direct physical, emotional or financial harm as the result of crimes or, in the case of murder, have lost an immediate family member. In his paper on 'The Implications for the Administration of Justice of the Victim Impact Statement Movement', Damian Bugg quotes from an essay by Dr Peter Grabosky:

> Until recently victims of crime have been considered the 'forgotten persons' of the Criminal Justice System . . . They report crimes to officials who decide whether to prosecute the case, how to proceed, and what type of punishment to recommend (where applicable). In adversary legal systems, such as Australia, England or the USA, the role of the victim in Court proceedings is a passive one—that of an observer or, at best, a witness . . . Victims

have no formally recognised role in the trial of their offender, and no mechanism to voice their concerns and feelings regarding the crime and its impact on them . . . (The) concept of crime as an offence against the State, and its attendant administration of justice, has resulted in a host of economic and psychological problems for crime victims, and most importantly, in perceptions of injustice. National movements concerned with ameliorating the victim's plights have emerged in numerous countries, including Australia.

Damian Bugg goes on to explain:

During the late 1970s and early 1980s the 'victim' movement gathered strength and in 1986 the General Assembly of the United Nations adopted and published the Basic Principles of Justice for Victims of Crime and Abuse of Power . . . The Principles attempted to define the basic rights or entitlements of victims in relation to criminal investigation, court proceedings and the provision of information. The Principles have commonly been called The Charter of Victims' Rights.

Fifteen rights are listed in this Charter, including: 'To be dealt with at all times in a sympathetic, constructive and reassuring manner with due regard to the victim's personal situation, rights and dignity.' Other rights are intended to ensure that every victim has access to information about the progress of the investigation—except where disclosure might jeopardise the investigation—about charges, the trial process, the rights and responsibilities of witnesses, about sentences and their implications. Still others relate to the protection of victims, especially where the accused applies for bail, and to the 'full effects of the crime upon him/her being made known to the sentencing court by the prosecutor in matters relating to offences of sexual assault or other personal violence'.

The Charter was adopted in Tasmania in 1991 and has Damian Bugg's support. At the same time, his sympathy for victims of crime is balanced by a determination to preserve the rights of the accused. He thinks the balance can be achieved by:

responsible observation of the requirements of the Charter, appropriate counselling and advice to victims, and appropriate statements by prosecuting authorities to the courts of the impact of the actual crime upon the victim or victims when the consequences or effects result from the specific criminal intent of the accused or were reasonably forseeable consequences of the accused's conduct.

That represents a fairly tall order for any Public Prosecutor in any case. But when the accused is charged with seventy-two crimes, including thirty-five murders, to maintain a balance between fairness to the accused and to the victims, provide those victims with appropriate counselling and advice and mount a case incorporating an appropriate victims' impact statement is a task to make anybody quail.

One of the first problems was to keep grief counsellors and agencies involved in the post-crisis management, and victims supplied with accurate information about the progress of events while avoiding any disclosure of information that might be seized on by the media and compromise Bryant's right to a fair trial.

Rod MacGregor, co-ordinator of the Port Arthur Incident Recovery Centre, helped by printing bulletins in *Port Arthur Update* but, as Damian Bugg pointed out, the difficulty remained:

> On the one hand, I was requiring the media to refrain from comment or speculation and on the other, I had to provide a flow of information which would assist various sections of the community, particularly the Peninsula, in understanding what was being done and what was likely to happen.

In early August the Police Department's Port Arthur Task Force passed their file of accumulated evidence to Damian Bugg and informed him that they were writing to all the people they had interviewed to let them know this had happened. The Director prepared a letter of his own, which was to go out with the Police communication, providing all interviewees with some basic information, and reassurance so that they were not cast adrift from the police with no indication of where the matter was heading.

This letter is a remarkable document. Lawyers have never had good press and government lawyers, in particular, are often seen as remote, pedantic and inhuman. Damian Bugg's letter, which went to about 750 people, is none of these. It answers questions such as who will give evidence and when witnesses will be required, and explains that he expects only a fraction of the many hundreds of people interviewed by police will be required as witnesses at Court for a trial. He also offers potential witnesses every possible assistance in the most sensitive terms imaginable:

> My office will consider . . . what inconveniences (travel, etc.) or stress will be caused to the witness, can it be avoided or lessened and is someone else available? . . . If you are to attend Court and you have any concerns then either my staff or I will discuss them with you, and, where necessary, take you to the Court building beforehand to familiarise you with the Court room itself.

And the help offered to potential witnesses did not end there:

> Bryant's appearance in Court and his plea to the Indictment was to take place on Monday, 30 September. I made arrangements to travel to Port Arthur on 24 September and be there to meet with a number of community representatives, health carers, Council officials at Nubeena and later to meet with staff and officials from the Port Arthur Historic Site . . . At the meetings I tried to outline what had occurred to date, where I thought the matter was proceeding and what was likely to happen in the event of both a plea of guilty and a plea of not guilty on 30 September . . . I hoped that many concerns, apprehensions and doubts could be dealt with, and at the same time I would avoid the risk of having the message

confused by being relayed through intermediaries . . .
People had an opportunity to come and speak to us
after the formal sessions and at least a less official face to
the Office of Director of Public Prosecutions was presented . . . I felt that it was important that everyone on the
Peninsula knew that I understood the concerns they
must have had about the pending trial and that every
consideration would be given to those concerns as we prepared for the trial.

On Monday, 30 September Bryant pleaded not guilty
to all charges and I am sure that this caused a consider-
able amount of anxiety and apprehension for those people
directly affected by Bryant's conduct. I settled on the
form of an appropriate insert for the *Port Arthur Update*
with Alex Schouten . . . My office then had to gear up
for a trial . . . and wrote to everybody, informing them
of either their acceptance or rejection as witnesses.

It was important that either Nick Perks, the Crown
Counsel, or I spoke directly to each of the non-Police
witnesses . . . We travelled to Melbourne on . . . 22
October to interview the thirty-eight Victorians we had
to call to give evidence . . . Nick flew on to Adelaide to
interview the twelve South Australian witnesses we would
be calling. I remained in Melbourne . . . I had hoped that
this process of direct contact would provide the witnesses
with a little encouragement and, hopefully, overcome
some of their fears of the 'unknown'.

We returned to Tasmania and commenced interview-
ing Tasmanian witnesses on 28 October . . . By this time
we had notified people employed at the Port Arthur

Historic Site that only four of their number were required
to give evidence but we also made ourselves available
for an afternoon meeting with Historic Site staff, counsellors, etc. to explain the Court process and the progress
of the trial . . . I must say that my experience from these
interviews was that, with very few exceptions, everyone,
both in Victoria and Tasmania, approached the task of
attending Court to give evidence with a positive
determination.

When Bryant pleaded guilty on 7 November, Nick Perks,
Craig Coad and Damian Bugg telephoned all the witnesses to
tell them they were no longer needed to give evidence, but
that if they wished to attend the sentencing hearing, Qantas
Airlines had offered discounted economy fares for all Port
Arthur victims and friends and family who travelled with them.

Meanwhile, the victims were invited to give details of the
various kinds of damage they had sustained as a result of
Bryant's crimes by contacting the Victims of Crime Service,
another body set up in response to the growing demand for
attention to victims' rights. All the statements were combined
to form a composite Victims' Impact Statement, which was
presented as a submission on the second day of the sentencing hearing by Damian Bugg. The Statement was
scrupulously fair to Bryant: it dealt only with effects which
resulted 'from the specific criminal intent of the accused or
were reasonably foreseeable consequences of the accused's conduct'. Yet the victims could feel that they had been allowed a
voice in the proceedings and the world, looking on, was
given some insight into the extent of the havoc which had

been wrought, of unspectacular suffering beyond the camera's range and lives changed forever by the events of the day.

Damian Bugg says:

> Through the whole process it was always my aim to ensure that people suffered as little trauma or anxiety as possible but at the same time I had to deal with matters in a factual way and not unfairly encourage people's expectations. There are many aspects of the trial process which are hard to understand, even for practising lawyers, and I regarded my role as encompassing a responsibility to adequately explain these procedures to people entitled to that explanation.

Damian Bugg was still explaining and answering questions at a meeting of victims, families, Port Arthur residents and counsellors on the second day of the hearing and again after the sentencing on 22 November. He had asked that Bryant should receive the maximum penalty for his crimes and that is the sentence which Chief Justice Cox handed down: on each of the thirty-five counts of murder, imprisonment for the term of the offender's natural life; on each of the remaining counts in the indictment, imprisonment for twenty-one years to be served concurrently with each other, and with the concurrent sentences of life imprisonment already imposed, with no eligibility for parole.

At the end of one of the meetings Damian Bugg addressed after the day's hearing, the crowd burst into applause. 'I think', he said, 'people were just relieved and there was some thanks for other people . . . I'm not prepared to say the round of applause was for the prosecution.' But it was—although it's impossible to tell whether the applause was for the way in which Damian Bugg had ensured that justice was done, for his compassion, or for his untiring efforts to demonstrate that compassion in every step he took.

~

Thousands of other people all over the world also tried to demonstrate compassion for the victims of the massacre. Messages of sympathy addressed to the

It was always my aim to ensure that people suffered as little trauma or anxiety as possible but at the same time I had to deal with matters in a factual way and not unfairly encourage people's expectations.

— DAMIAN BUGG

Tasmanian Premier or the Mayor of Tasman or occasionally, the Mayor of Tasmania, came flooding in. The people of Dunblane sent a public message of condolence through their provost, John Paterson, followed by advice from their community co-ordinator on key issues such as communication, co-ordination, trusts and memorials. At Port Arthur, Craig Coomb's first telephone call on 16 May came from the Vatican. A message from His Holiness, which was to be read at the Sunday memorial service, was about to arrive.

The Premier's Department stepped in to provide help at the Tasman Council Chambers. Neil Noye and the Council's General Manager, Greg Burgess, were there on the morning of 29 April answering media calls from all over Australia, and the world. 'We were really the only two running it', says Neil. 'The telephone lines were jammed up till 11.00 p.m. It was full-on for the first week or ten days until such time as we got a media officer there to assist.' Neighbouring Councils also helped by lending staff and Sorell Council provided Tasman with a Commander Telephone System.

Newsletters, distributed to Peninsula residents in the days after 28 April, are full of acknowledgements of a bewildering range of gifts or other forms of assistance:

> Tasmanian musicians are getting behind next Sunday's Family Picnic and Music Day at Port Arthur in a big way. More than 70 will be at the Historic Site throughout the day to provide a smorgasbord of music for picnickers. And they will be offering their talent free-of-charge as a helping hand to get the Tasman Peninsula up and running again . . .

> Yachts from this year's Sydney–Hobart fleet will take part in a memorial cruise to Port Arthur at the end of the race. The cruise will have a twofold purpose: to honour the memory of the Port Arthur shooting victims and to acknowledge the role the port has played over the years as a safe haven for yachts . . .

> Electronic commerce expert, Manny Spiteri . . . is working hard to get the Peninsula on the Internet by the end of this week, having acquired a free web site for a year . . . Manny said the Internet would prove a powerful worldwide promotional tool for the Peninsula's tourist industry . . .

> People closely affected by the Port Arthur tragedy are being offered holiday breaks in the Great Lakes District of

New South Wales in September. The offer has come from the seaside community of Forster–Tuncurry, which has been moved by the events of 28 April to set up a 'Sharing the Caring' Appeal. Tourism operators in the district have got together to offer a week's holiday at minimum expense to those in need of a break. The offer includes free accommodation, reduced-cost transport and reduced-cost activities in the Great Lakes region . . .

Wayne Edwards, an art teacher from Tasmania's north-west, provided an opportunity for anyone affected by the massacre to express their feelings in a way that would be heard, but which avoided the stress of engaging with the media. He let it be known that he was collecting together writing, music and painting which people had produced in an attempt to cope with their grief, and went on to stage an exhibition at the Showcase Gallery in Devonport. It was called 'The Twenty-Eighth of April—An exhibition of immediate personal responses to the Port Arthur massacre'. Mervyn and Mary Howard's children wrote, offering a poem; a relative of Glenn Pears sent another; the mother of a nurse who had been on duty at the hospital up until midnight on 28 April and again at 7.30 the next day, contributed a piece which ends:

Later in 'Burns', with sickencd minds
And faces carved from stone,
They mutely accept a new admission.

'The individual journeys of bereavement', said Wayne Edwards, 'have had many manifestations; the questioning has been echoed throughout the nation. This questioning of life and death, of good and evil, has allowed bonds to develop which under normal circumstances would never have taken place'.

And so it went on, with people offering aid of every sort: from air-fares to a holiday destination for someone in need of a break to the Hobart City Mission's emergency relief of food and clothing for Peninsula residents facing hardship.

On 29 April, the Premier of Tasmania announced the establishment of a Port Arthur Victims' Appeal Fund and primed the pump with a government contribution of $100,000. The Fund was to provide compensation for the dependants of those killed at Port Arthur, the injured and their dependants; to meet emergency costs like funerals or the fares of relatives coming to visit the wounded in hospital; and to cover direct costs arising as a consequence of the events which are not recoverable from other sources. These might include shortfalls in medical expenses for injured victims, loss of income, and support for people living in the Tasman Council area.

The money came from the Federal Government, the governments of other Australian states, banks, sporting clubs, a publisher, a TV network and thousands of private citizens. A song-writer and singer contributed the proceeds from the sale of a CD; a group of children in an after school-care program raised $1400 by making and selling guardian angel fridge magnets; choirs combined to give a fund-raising concert. A committee made up of Henry Cosgrove, a former judge, Bob Grierson from the Premier's Department, and the Mayor of Tasman, Neil Noye, was given the task of allocating the funds, and called on Legal Aid to help applicants make their claims. The committee arranged for each person to be interviewed by a Legal Aid officer, agreeing that a direct, personal approach would be less traumatic and more efficient.

In late June the committee reported that victims had proved reluctant to make claims. But, despite this, it was already clear that there would not be enough money to provide them with appropriate compensation. Already, the committee had paid out close to $300,000 for funeral and travelling expenses. Further payments were stopped until after the end of October when applications were to close and

This questioning of life and death, of good and evil, has allowed bonds to develop which under normal circumstances would never have taken place.

— WAYNE EDWARDS

the task of divvying up the remaining funds would begin. Meanwhile the committee chairman urged that 'all applicants to the fund must, if they can, apply for Criminal Injuries Compensation', payment made through the Supreme Court to approved victims who have suffered loss, injury or expense as the result of a crime. The hope was that pressure could be taken off the Victims' Appeal Fund by ensuring that applicants exhausted all other avenues of compensation first, such as workers' compensation, private life insurance benefits, and Criminal Injuries Compensation, which, in Tasmania, provides payments of up to $20,000.

By November 1996 almost $3.25 million had been contributed to the Appeal Fund. 'In the last months', said the Premier, 'although we have seen the worst of human behaviour we have also seen the very best. It makes me very proud to be part of the Australian nation, to see the support, the donations to the appeal fund. I am very pleased we are part of a very civilised and caring nation.'

But, as Henry Cosgrove pointed out, the victims of the massacre were by no means all part of that nation. Some lived in Switzerland, South Africa, Malaysia, Canada and the USA. And of the Australian victims, most came from states other than Tasmania. 'The bounty of the fund,' he said, 'must be spread between all these places.'

> *In the last months, although we have seen the worst of human behaviour, we have also seen the very best.*
>
> — TONY RUNDLE

In the end, it was spread rather less thinly than he feared because just before Christmas the Supreme Court ruled that part of Bryant's assets, worth over $1 million, should be forfeited to the state. It also signalled in January that his share in the estate of George Adams—a further $600,000 or so—was to go the same way. The Federal Government added to the money available for Bryant's victims by waiving some $250,000 worth of income tax on his fortune. Now, the fortune that enabled Martin Bryant to indulge his taste for buying expensive firearms has been placed in a special trust account for the benefit of his victims.

Martin Bryant had not been born wealthy, but in 1987 he had met Helen Mary Harvey, one of the beneficiaries in the will of George Adams, the founder of Tattersall's lotteries. He started doing odd jobs for Miss Harvey, gradually became her companion and, when she died in 1992, inherited her house in New Town, a small farm, and her share in the Adams' estate.

Not all the financial contributions that came in the wake of the shooting went to the Appeal Fund. According to Neil Noye, the Tasman Council had been forced to foot a sizeable bill in terms of telephone costs and salaries, which was becoming a real burden on the ratepayers. But Sorell Council and the State Government both chipped in and paid the greater part of these expenses.

Still more government aid came from Tasmania Development and Resources. In December Neil Noye reported:

We . . . contacted the Premier's Department and Tasmania Development and Resources (TDR) to get them into the district and circulating around. Port Arthur started to recover after that initial three-week period . . . it wasn't only tourism—the people of Tasmania really got behind it and that was excellent for Port Arthur itself. That was coming back nicely.

But then at the fringes, at the caravan parks, the holiday homes and other accommodation, these were really hurting . . . After I contacted the Premier, the loan assistance started to come through. Overall we have had a tremendous amount of assistance from the Government and from various Departments.

Some came from the Federal Government in the form of funding for courses for the owners and employees of small businesses on the Peninsula. As Neil explains further, 'The Prime Minister also allocated $2.5 million specifically for the Port Arthur Historic Site. Many people thought that the assistance from the Federal Government was for the community, but it wasn't—it was given to the Historic Site to rebuild the Visitors' Centre and to upgrade the car-park.'

From the point of view of some tourist operators this was an excellent idea. The number of visitors to Port Arthur has increased since 28 April, but the popularity of the evening ghost tours has fallen by 30 per cent. People aren't staying overnight. Michael Kelley, who runs one of the best seafood restaurants in Australia in a wooded park close to the toll-booth, has had his worst summer ever. As he sees it: 'People just come down for the day and go back to Hobart so we're not getting the trade. Something's got to be done quickly. We can't go on like this.'

The Port Arthur Management Board are planning to stage an evening sound and light show in the new Visitors' Centre which might help to keep tourists on the Peninsula for more than a day. But not everyone sees the matter in this way. Some feel that, once again, the Board has appropriated some-thing which perhaps should go to the Tasman community.

∾

Martin Bryant put an end to many relationships between peo-ple and, through the stress and altered circumstances he created, damaged many more. So it was, perhaps, predictable that in the first weeks after the shooting much of the recovery work on the Peninsula should have been concerned with trying to safe-guard or repair fundamental connections between human beings, with small groups of neighbours, families and individ-uals reaching out to help each other.

Alan and Annie Andrews, having moved into Brigid Cook's house to look after her children, coped with a stream of journalists, well-wishers and local people who called in because they felt a need to talk. Mark Kirby arrived with the purpose of fixing her driveway:

Brigid had been leaving her car at the bottom and walking up. That was impossible now because of the injuries to her legs, so I made some phone calls and through the kindness of a couple of people in particular I had her driveway fixed for nothing. One from out Salt Water River did the excavation work and the other put about three loads of gravel in for nothing. No pay at all. After that . . . I went up with David Scott, Conservation Manager at the Port Arthur Site, and we did the quantities for what she'd need to have the interior lining put in her house. I had a good friend at Kemp and Denning's in town . . . I rang them up and asked them what they could do for us and they said, 'We'll do what we can for you. Not a problem'. So we sent them a list . . . In the end, after some negotiation, K and D paid for what we needed and I went up and spent a week up there doing some work to the house.

As Alan says:

The community became like an organism. We acted as a body. We were called upon to deal with a situation and nobody really stopped to think. They just did it. I saw some of the best of people during that time. There was a rushing . . . it was like the corpuscles to a wound . . . I felt in communion with people in a way that I very rarely feel.

Catie Porteous, who had worked at the Site as an apprentice gardener, felt much the same. When she went to visit her former workmates she was moved by the open way in which they spoke to her:

I don't know if they wanted to talk to me like that or if they just couldn't help themselves, but it was wonderful. I felt much closer to them than I'd ever felt before. It's made me feel differently about people, made me value them more, especially my parents.

Peter Rigozzi and his partner, Heather, have a composite family of four children: two of his and two of hers. Like many other parents they spent a lot of time helping their children come to terms with what had happened:

My youngest was totally traumatised at first. He was crying and I couldn't quite work out why—whether it was because the people had been shot or what it was. It turned out he was afraid this man was going to come and get us . . . but he, having had the strongest initial reaction of . . . fear for the safety of the family, actually grasped the reality of the situation very quickly whereas . . . some of the others took days and weeks to really grasp it . . . We do have a fairly open household when it comes to discussing stuff and Heather, being a nurse, has always been interested in grief and dying and palliative care and those sort of processes. She has a much more— I'd probably have to say—naturally caring and nurturing attitude than I do and I think she does it very well . . . My approach is 'Well, there are people out there in a terrible mess, people who've lost relatives and everything and who really need understanding and help, but we need to be thankful, really, that none of us have actually been shot . . . We are very fortunate'. Heather talks with them much more about the issues involved and the feelings involved and that sort of thing. Between the two of us—and the kids speak fairly freely as well—we got through pretty well. It did obviously affect them but they weren't waking up screaming in a sweat or anything like that and for that we are very thankful.

> *The community became like an organism . . . I felt in communion with people in a way that I very rarely feel.*
>
> — ALAN ANDREWS

As President of the School Council, Peter had a special interest in how the school coped with the impact of the massacre:

Considering that nobody at the school has anything of this magnitude to deal with on a daily, yearly or lifetime basis, I think that they actually did remarkably well. Many of the counsellors who came down to the Peninsula focused on the school. The school . . . is like a reflection of the community. It has a very close feel. Even though there's a continual staff turn-over it's quite a tight-knit school, I think, and it remained so through the initial days of the whole process. There was a unanimous feeling in the school that they wanted nothing to do with the media. There was a very protective feeling towards the kids because, of course, some of the kids—and some of the staff—had very direct involvement. So the media were kept right away from the school . . . and consequently, because the school was encapsulated and protected and was crawling with counsellors, I think it did very well. I think there was a very quick recovery process in the school. I mean, obviously, it's still on-going and it's still on-going in a private fashion really.

A more detailed picture of the kind of distress that the school had to cope with in the first days of the massacre comes from a staff member who was there on 30 April:

I was walking past the Home Ec. room when suddenly I heard my name being called. It was the Home Ec. teacher's aide. 'Quick, quick', she yelled, 'come and help me with these girls—they're all falling to pieces.' With that they came streaming out of the room crying hysterically—some more than others. I put one arm around one group and my other arm around another, trying to pacify them. 'Why did he have to do it? Why did he have to do it?' they sobbed, working themselves into quite a frenzy. I must admit my throat felt very tight as I tried to quell my own tears, which any minute could have taken over—so grief-stricken and bewildered were these children.

Fortunately the school was overflowing with counsellors and I quickly ran looking for one of them. I remember as I was running, my tears spilled over and the full magnitude of the disaster hit me and I kept thinking, 'How can we ordinary people ever possibly deal with all of this?' My colleague had managed to move the group into another room by the time I got back with a counsellor who had grabbed bags of Minties and sweet biscuits. He handed these out to the girls and we went off to make mugs of hot sweet tea.

All across the Peninsula other groups were drawing together to provide mutual aid and support. John Hamilton, realising that the dissemination of accurate information is of particular importance in any disaster-stricken community, enlisted the aid of several people so that he could print and distribute a news-sheet.

We thought we were close as a group before, now we are able to openly 'bare our souls' to each other and gain much support.

— ELAINE BALL

Father Morgan Batt, the Catholic priest whose parish includes the Tasman Peninsula, telephoned Father Basil O'Sullivan of Dunblane to ask his advice. The answer was: 'Gather your community and pray'. Other church groups were doing exactly the same and, in some cases, reaching out to those around them by offering counselling. Alan Imber is one of the Anglican congregation who tried to help in this way. Elaine Ball managed to set up weekly meetings of Community Health workers to provide a 'time of sharing our experiences and giving support to each other'. In August she wrote: 'We thought we were close as a group before, now we are able to openly "bare our souls" to each other and gain much support.' She also established a Community Link Group to bring people from different parts of the Peninsula together.

John Hillman, a former bank manager who has been selling real estate for the past twelve years, is the President of the local Rotary Club whose members have also drawn closer together in the wake of the shooting. The club was being formed, and was ready to be chartered in June, when the massacre happened.

When the massacre happened at Port Arthur on the Sunday . . . as President I didn't think anyone would be interested in going to a Rotary meeting on Wednesday. Many of our members like Pam and Steve Ireland, Walter Mikac, Paul Hyland, all were involved . . . I was about to cancel it and then they started to phone me and say that they wanted to meet. So I phoned the Fox and Hounds, our regular meeting place, to see if they were operational . . . they said 'Yes'. They were fine and there was nobody about anyway . . . Then I got a call from Sorell, who are our sponsor club. Seven of them wanted to come down and spend the evening with us. So we met. There were close to thirty of us there that night and it was the most incredible meeting. We had someone from the mainland to do with the Uniting Church and Glenn Cumbers from the Church of Christ here. And they spoke about the day and different things. I dispensed with the normal format of the meeting and just let it go and it was a case of people just talking about it. And it was the most incredible experience . . . and through that it drew everybody together as a club.

And the next stage was to be actually chartered. Through what happened we were suddenly in the spotlight not only in Australia but worldwide. We got faxes and letters from all over Australia and overseas. When it came to the charter night—normally you'd have about 100 people, I suppose—and we were going to have it down here, naturally. Then it came through that it looked as though we'd have 300 plus people that wanted to come from throughout Australia and everywhere. We checked round and they couldn't cater for those sort of numbers down here . . . . we really didn't want to turn away all these people and a lot of money was coming in that we could use for the community. We got about $20,000 given to us for the charter by other clubs and that was only the beginning. So in the end I was able to convince the members that we should go up to town to the Casino. The other thought was that we were living with it continually at that time . . . people like Pam and Steve were pretty strung out. We thought if we got away from it we could have a night out in town. There were over 300 people at the Casino. It was an incredible night. Everybody had a ball. Then . . . more money came in. To date around $45,000 has come in from other clubs. So then we had to decide what we would do with the money . . . In the end we thought we'd look to the future, the kids. What we've got now is two scholarships: one for Grade 10 and one for tertiary. And that will be an on-going thing with the interest from the money. Hopefully it will build up and we'll maybe have another scholarship or even four scholarships . . . Since then we've had our own projects going. We gave a trailer to the school. They need that for going away on camps . . . It's a very strong club . . . I always remember Pam Ireland saying to me she felt it was weird that it just seemed to happen at that time we were formed as a club (when) it happened at Port Arthur, and with all the money that came in and the expertise within the club we were able to help.

The Tasman Lions Club also swung into action and decided to throw their weight behind a local committee that had been trying to raise the money to build a Community Hall or Entertainment Centre at Nubeena. 'This', they announced, 'is to be an effective memorial to the residents of the Tasman Peninsula who lost their lives in the Port Arthur massacre on the 28 April 1996, not forgetting also the many visitors who suffered the same tragic fate'.

The land for the building has been donated by the Tasman Council, led by Neil Noye. More than any other body, the Council co-ordinated and stimulated the work of recovery on the Peninsula. Greg Burgess, the General Manager, explains that the Council itself is one of the smallest in Tasmania.

We have an administrative and technical staff of seven and an outside workforce of the same number . . .

There we were, plunged into the world spotlight, for all the wrong reasons, having to take responsibility for co-ordination of the recovery process, deal with the media and try to keep the affairs of the municipality 'on track'. To say it was 'tough' and still is would be an understatement.

As well as coping with a torrent of enquiries, gifts and messages of sympathy, and setting up support systems for the counsellors and other relief workers who were coming into the municipality, the Council was intent on recovery from inside. 'We were happy,' says Neil Noye, 'to accept help from outside, but the main effort and direction had to come from us.'

> *We were happy to accept help from outside, but the main effort and direction had to come from us.*
>
> — NEIL NOYE

He visited all the local people who had lost loved ones, attended funerals and simply listened to those who wanted to talk. The Council established a Community Newsletter, which was distributed twice a week to every household in the area. This contained details about what the Council was doing, and asked for residents' input. 'It was probably the most beneficial thing that we did for the community. They wanted news and the information was critical.'

One of the most important pieces of information carried by the first newsletter concerned the setting up of a Recovery Task Force or Community Recovery Working Party made up of the Mayor and Deputy Mayor (Peter Wilson of the Frances Langford Tea Rooms), Craig Coombs, Ian Kingston, Elaine

Ball, Steve Ireland, Terry Polglase (school principal) and several others. Its meetings were open and everyone had the chance to vote on any issue. 'Those that were uptight', says Neil, 'or were in some way affected by the tragedy needed to be given something to do.' The Task Force therefore formed a number of subcommittees: the Memorial Committee, the Trust Fund Committee and the Special Events Committee. 'We found that where people wanted to be involved we gave them a committee job—where they weren't satisfied, we gave them two committees to be involved with to keep them occupied.'

But the subcommittees served more than a therapeutic purpose. The Memorial Committee, chaired by Pam Ireland, was formed to collate suggestions and information concerning a memorial at Port Arthur more permanent than Mick McMillan's cross.

The Trust Fund Committee was created as a fund-raising body which, once the Victims' Appeal Fund closed, would continue receiving money for projects and developments that benefit the Tasman Community. Already money has come in from a 'Spirit of Tamworth' concert and from a celebrity cricket match that the Special Events Committee helped to organise.

The Trust has an opportunity to do something new which both honours the victims of the massacre and revitalises the local economy. The Tasman Peninsula could become an international symbol for what can be done in the face of disaster, for bringing life out of death. After the bushfires at Mount Macedon in Victoria a college was established to study the causes and management of disasters. After the Port Arthur tragedy the Tasman Peninsula could become a place dedi-

cated to renewal, to a process of regrowth in which everyone who comes here could participate.

The Trust is considering a series of projects connected with
physical growth, among them: a 1940s-style orchard run like
one of the properties which made the Peninsula prosperous fifty
years ago, a place where visitors can join in the work, taste
varieties of apples which are fast disappearing, buy cider and
apple brandy and stay on; a vineyard planted in honour of
Jason Winter, the young winemaker who died in the Broad
Arrow; and a great garden, incorporating a section dedicated
to flowers and shrubs with special uses—a project in which
a benefactor has already shown interest. And then there are
projects concerned with renewal and growth of a different
kind. Port Arthur is surrounded by sites which have never
been excavated—the boys' prison at Point Puer, for example—and much of its history, along with that of the convicts who
were imprisoned there, remains to be explored. The place
deserves to become an international centre for historical studies, just as the whole Peninsula deserves to attract the attention
of conservationists and artists from all over the world.

This all needs careful management. As Peter MacFie warns:

The danger is we are losing what we revere in Tasmania
while still trying to come to terms with and unravel the past
and our own attitudes to it. We are being pressured to
grasp a gimmick here and a yarn there to draw more
and more tourists, but there is a great danger we will
swamp the goose that lays the golden eggs. As unemployment and financial pressures push Australians to seek

meaning from the past, there is a danger that the past will be ransacked instead.

Much the same might be said about the environment. It's tempting to envisage a future in which a mini-campus is established near Koonya where students can study the preservation of both historic sites and rainforest; marine ecology; painting; music. There might be master classes, conferences and weekend seminars, all of which would ensure that the local shops stay open, the accommodation businesses keep running and more young people stay in the district. But if this very special place is to become more widely known for growth or renewal of this kind we shall have to be careful that the natural beauty of its beaches and mountains—the very asset which makes it so attractive to conservationists and artists— is not, as the poet Les Murray once said, 'humanised to death'. So the Trust has its work cut out and so, too, does the Special Events Committee.

As time went on two further groups grew up under the Council's wing: the Port Arthur and Tasman Region Visitors' Association and the Tasman Community Broadcasters. By December 1996 the Visitors' Association had secured the appointment of a tourism, marketing and development officer, set up an information centre at Eaglehawk Neck and started work on the production of new maps and brochures. Tasman Community Broadcasters have tested possible transmission sites and aim to have a radio station on-air by or soon after the first anniversary of the shooting in April 1997.

∽

As well as overseeing the establishment of the various sub-committees which developed from the original taskforce, the Mayor set off, shortly after the shooting, on a whistle-stop tour of Australia with the Chairman of the Port Arthur Authority and the Premier. The tour was intended in part to raise morale or heal wounds but also had a practical purpose. Greg Burgess explains:

> What became apparent very early was that the community would soon face a second disaster if immediate action was not taken. That second disaster was the potential collapse of the economic base of the area, which is principally based on tourism. Understandably people were staying away and cancellations were reported from all quarters. There was an urgent need to get the message out to Australia that, whilst we had suffered this enormous tragedy, the area was safe, was still as scenic and as beautiful as ever, and all the features, both natural and man-made, which attracted people to the area, were still here.

So, in the intervals between thanking the people of Australia because they had been marvellous, meeting with the families of mainland victims and accepting donations to the Appeal Fund, the Tasmanian delegation kept spreading the word that tourists were needed in the Island State—and especially in Tasman—as never before.

Through all this Neil Noye refused to claim any costs or out-of-pocket expenses even though he had to neglect his business and his farm for months at a time.

One very important aspect of the Council involvement was the tremendous part played by Greg Burgess, the General Manager, and Barry Chandler, the Accountant. They each put in extremely long hours each day, all week, and they didn't once give in. We gave Greg a fortnight off for the time he had put in, but all during this he kept coming into the office every day to ensure that things were going properly. There was no asking for overtime, or only working to fixed hours. Many nights we were there till well after midnight—as long as it took to do what we had to do.

PACE (Peninsula Action for Community Enterprise), which has its offices in a cottage that was once part of the Impression Bay Probation Station at Premaydena, near Glen Imber's shop, did what it could to support the Council and some of its sub-committees. As well as offering its usual services to local small businesses—information, advice, word-processing, photo-copying and so on—it provided some training facilities for those wanting to acquire computer skills, supported other training programs and served as a base for visiting officers from the Department of Social Services and the Commonwealth Employment Service. Its Co-operative Society developed gardens at the school and around the PACE cottage, built up a tool pool and sold produce at the Saturday markets in Hobart's Salamanca Place.

Since 28 April, PACE has organised two important conferences: a Search Conference in June and a Youth Conference in August. Both gave residents an opportunity to come together to work out what could be done to make the future of the

Peninsula community more hopeful and secure. There was a good feeling at the conference in June, a sense that people were emerging from grief and shock, ready to make plans and work together to get the place back on its feet.

A month later Peter Rigozzi gave a party to celebrate the completion of his new workshop—a large shed, which on that chilly night in July was full of trestle tables laden with food and drink, and crowds of people dancing to the music of a local band. Outside there was a bonfire. Children ran in and out. The Campbells were there, Brigid Cook, the Langleys . . . It seemed, we all thought, that the worst was behind us.

At Port Arthur a new café had been built on to one side of the Broad Arrow and Brigid had been made the manager. 'We're just getting on with our life and I'm reclaiming my space,' she said. 'I'm happy to be back at work and this is a good place to be.'

Neil Noye saw the annual revue staged in the school hall in September as a turning point: 'It brought the house down with laughter . . . Walter Mikac was in it, and Nicole Burgess' mother did the make-up and her father helped as well.' The Council news-sheet hailed the show as a 'a hit' which 'packed in the patrons' and raised over $2,000 for the Pool Committee and the Hall Committee. The comic team of Steve Ireland, Eddie Halton, Guy Dobner and Walter Mikac stole the show with their impression of Abba in drag.

> *Port Arthur is not just a story about death. It is also a story about life and how precious it is. It is not just a story about tragedy. It is also a story about triumph. Triumph of the human spirit.*
>
> — *MERCURY*

When Bryant pleaded not guilty and it looked, for a time, as though there would be a trial that went on for up to five weeks, the atmosphere in Tasman grew more tense. But once the plea was changed and the sentencing hearing had come and gone, many of us believed all would be well. The *Mercury*, now free to print what it liked, carried a batch of stories 'we can now tell you' and announced: 'Port Arthur is not just a story about death. It is also a story about life and how precious it is. It is not just a story about tragedy. It is also a story about triumph. Triumph of the human spirit.'

And so we learnt, amongst much else, that Linda White, the patient the Dells had met at the Fox and Hounds, was slowly recovering from the injury to her arm and that she and Michael Wanders, her boyfriend, meant to get married on 28 April 1997. As Linda explained in a television interview, Bryant had tried to kill her and had failed, so she felt she had triumphed over him.

By Christmas those of us on the fringes, who had no intimate contact with anyone who had been permanently damaged by the day, were sure that soon everything would be all right again. We were sorry that Walter had gone and that Steve Ireland had suddenly left the Peninsula, but, all in all, we thought that once the holidays came and the tourist operators began to recover their losses, the community would return, if not to normal, to something very like what it had been before. Perhaps, in the end, things might even be better.

Then, suddenly, in the middle of a glorious summer, Port Arthur was back in the headlines. The Board, to do it justice, had worked hard to alleviate the effects of the day. It had begun by calling a meeting of staff immediately after the

massacre and had gone on to deploy a series of officers spe-
cially charged with dealing with the problems encountered
by the workforce. Michael Langley was appointed as head of
a 'short-term issues committee', established to tackle issues
related to 28 April. John Edwards, the Rehabilitation Co-ordinator, joined the team. A Media Office was set up, and when
Colonel Woodland of the Salvation Army reported that for
some 'the cocoon of protection that was put in place . . . has
been allowed to develop into a cocoon of "isolation"', an inde-
pendent liaison officer was appointed.

Attempts were made to improve relations between the management of the Site and the community. Craig Coombs, the
General Manager, joined at least half-a-dozen local committees. Michael Mazengarb appeared at a number of meetings, like
the one that heralded the establishment of the Tasman Trust.
Neil Noye was invited to join the Board after he had pointed
out in his speech to the Search Conference that the only
Tasman resident among the Board's member—though well
respected—was chosen by the Board and not by the people of
the Peninsula. And a Community Outreach Officer was appointed to attempt the building of bridges between the Site's
management team and the local population.

A great deal of work was done to try to bring back tourists
to Port Arthur and to hurry on the building of the new Visitors'
Centre, and the launching of the promised sound and light
show. In the meantime ghost tours were re-introduced, first
as 'evening tours', then under their old title. After all, the Site
was the region's biggest employer and the king-pin in its set of
tourist attractions. Unless the show kept rolling, Tasman, as
Greg Burgess had feared, would suffer a second disaster and

everyone struggling out of the trauma of the massacre would be traumatised all over again. Yet, though this argument may have seemed self-evident to the Board, there were many ready to challenge it, and still more who resented the idea that it could be true.

The first concerted attack on the Port Arthur Historic Site Management Authority came under the banner headline, 'Ruination'. The issue was an old one: Andrew Piper, a former Conservation Manager, claimed that the historic buildings were being shamefully neglected, that funds for their preservation were inadequate and no proper program of conservation had been put in place. He was supported by, among others, Dr Brian Egloff, a specialist in cultural heritage management, who had been at Port Arthur in the days of the conservation project. According to Dr Egloff:

When the Port Arthur Project was winding down, we were seeking to determine how the Government was going to deal with a site into which $9 million of public funds had been invested. Their response was to form the Management Authority in order for the site to become self-funding. That was dreadfully irresponsible on the part of Government. A historic resource is expensive to maintain and to expect that site to earn enough money to maintain itself and to provide visitors with a reasonable experience is literally unheard of in terms of historic site management . . . By taking that extremely ill-advised action, a series of events was set in train which led to over-commercialism.

Politicians entered the fray, calling for an immediate inquiry, and an accountant employed by the Port Arthur Historic Site Management Authority has brought a case against the Management Authority for breach of contract. This introduced a second issue.

In its single-minded pursuit of the tourist dollar—or of apparent success in catching it—had the Board neglected staff as well as buildings? This, too, was not a new issue and soon the air was thick with complaints. Some of it seemed unfair. The Board had, after all, made attempts to help its staff in the aftermath of the massacre and if, as Michael Langley has pointed out, it was slow in ensuring that their efforts on the day were fully acknowledged, it had tried

The trouble lay, perhaps, not so much in what was done but in how it was done.

hard ever since to make up for lost time. Michael Mazengarb responded: 'We have worked our butts off and done what we thought was our very best and now we are being crucified for it.'

The trouble lay, perhaps, not so much in what was done but in how it was done. Some believe that it would have been better if the Board had written to the local community in the way Damian Bugg did, and met with them repeatedly as a group. One employee said, 'Most of us don't even know who they all are.' In some cases, the staff feel very much like the convicts who once worked where they work. They wear uniforms; some of them—like some of the convict workforce—prepare food, tend gardens, lay bricks, clean up. Their bosses, until recently, were housed in Civil Row on the slope overlooking the oval and take their orders, in turn, from a faceless power in Hobart. On top of this, some staff are descended from convicts and from citizens of Carnarvon, from people who made the prison into a free town.

All this, which affects attitudes in the Tasman community as well as on the Site itself, lay behind the next two assaults launched on the Board. The first was an attack on the new Visitors' Centre and the planned sound and light show. There was a public meeting, an attempt to get a Supreme Court injunction and a flurry of threats followed by a police investigation. At much the same time two former members of staff, both of whom had been much affected by the events of 28 April, began calling for an inquiry into security at the Site and into the locking of the gift-shop door through which, they claimed, seven of those who died might have escaped to safety.

The Minister responsible for the Site has since ruled out the possibility of an inquiry into the massacre and gradually the fury raised by the recent disputes is cooling a little, but recovery in Tasman has slowed. The gift-shop door was made of glass and, in the event of a fire or almost any emergency other than a hail of bullets, could have been smashed, but those concerned with security and maintenance at the Site are now raking their consciences all over again. The summer has not proved as profitable as many hoped, so that some tourist operators are angry at the threat to the sound and light show, which might, they believe, keep them in business. At the moment it's all too easy to feel that the massacre of 28 April has left a legacy of anger, grief and despair that will never be dissipated, that the beauty and peace of the Peninsula are permanently blighted and its community divided. But when one looks more closely another picture begins to emerge.

Peter Rigozzi sometimes wonders if there is something wrong with him because he can still wake up in the morning and say, 'What a spot!'

> The Peninsula is not ruined forever for me.
> Nothing in essence has changed. There's been an
> awful disaster and there are people grieving
> who are directly involved but as far as the
> Peninsula itself is concerned it's still the
> same as it was. The sun still rises in
> the morning. It's still a beautiful place.

And he still believes in a future for his children. When you go to the school in Nubeena it becomes clear that he is not alone in this. The school has come a long way since last year. Building work has been completed. There are fresh, well-lit spaces, and a new library equipped with computers giving access to both the Internet and the catalogue of the entire State collection from which users can order books. The most innovative feature of the library is that it serves the whole local community as well as the school. Because older people now visit the school regularly to borrow books and rub shoulders with the students, there is growing interest in what 'our school' is doing and more support for its activities, while, in turn, the students are meeting more adult residents and developing a clearer sense of the community in which they live.

The principal, Terry Polglase, foresees a time when the aged from the nursing home down the road will come to the library to read stories to the younger children or be read to by the older ones. He also has plans to establish a website on the internet and access learning programmes from across the world by satellite so that, for young and old alike, many disadvantages of living in a place as remote as the Tasman Peninsula will be overcome.

Another new project in which students from the Tasman District School are involved is the development of the Green House community centre. This has nothing to do with plants and everything to do with growth of a different kind. The Green House, donated to the community by the Uniting Church, has become the meeting-place for recovery and self-help groups like Elaine Ball's Community Health workers, but above all for a new Youth Group which voiced its needs at the Youth Conference organised by PACE and is now working to achieve its goals.

> *The people who are pressing on with these projects would be surprised to hear themselves described as 'strong' or 'courageous'. They see themselves as simply getting on with their lives.*

The people who are pressing on with these projects would be surprised to hear themselves described as 'strong' or 'courageous'. They see themselves as simply getting on with their lives. Some, perhaps, are inspired by the memory of how things were in the weeks immediately after the massacre when, as Alan Andrews has described, everyone drew together to offer each other support. That memory has certainly remained with the artisan in wood Peter Adams, who wrote the following letter in May 1996:

In January of this year, beneath the shade of a wattle tree on the lawns of the Tasman Municipal Council offices, I took the oath to become an Australian citizen.

Now, more than ever, I feel I made the right decision.

Without a doubt, these past few weeks have been testing—on my sense of purpose, my understanding of life and death, and the values I place on humanity—but what has emerged is a stronger sense of self within a stronger community.

Two things have worked together to achieve this: the healing powers of nature and a community in heartfelt action to redress a terrible wrong.

To walk along the wildness of Roaring Beach, stand within the delicateness of a she-oak grove or happen upon an ant-searching echidna is to be in the presence of God. And this is comforting, life-enforcing.

To have as your neighbours a community of caring, loving people working together selflessly to reweave the wholeness is to learn compassion, know humility without feeling insignificant, and to come away with an honest pride that is deeply grateful that this place is called home.

∼

Last night I sat with Naomi on my front verandah overlooking the glimmering expanse of Princes Bay. We agreed that behind all the recent troubles lies the central question of how we see the past and that there will never be lasting peace until we recognise the wrongs that have been done, the horrors that have been perpetrated, without pretence or exaggeration. We cannot pretend that the convict experience or the massacre never happened but neither can we see the men who created the convict system or Martin Bryant as so vile that they are no longer human beings.

Naomi said:

We need to try to understand what made them like they were—or are. If we just push them away it might all happen again. We've got to have an honest relationship with the past or we'll never get our heads right, we'll never know who we are. And we'll never get the tourism thing right either because we won't have anything real to show the tourists. At least we've got to get them looking at real questions about how they see the convicts—and how they see us, living here on the Peninsula.

After Naomi had gone home I sat on for a long time in the darkness. I believe what she had said is quite true, but I wished that I had said to her that the inevitable accompaniment of honestly facing cruelty and pain is an equivalent recognition of compassion and courage. These qualities come often in such ordinary forms that you may not recognise them but they are there all the same: in the people of the Broad Arrow, in everyone who has worked and struggled to overcome the effects of the massacre, in the community where it occurred. Finally,

I remembered some words spoken at a memorial service in Hobart on the Friday after the shooting.

We have choices between shutting doors and opening them, between withdrawal and advance. Some people have said recently that they will never eat in a restaurant again, never go for a Sunday drive . . . But there is, as it were, a flip side to this fear. Perhaps we do well to remember that we are never absolutely safe, that some freakish event might strike us down—or those we love—at any moment. But one outcome of that is to live each day as if it were our last and to value those who are dear to us more highly.

Behind all the recent troubles lies the central question of how we see the past and that there will never be lasting peace until we recognise the wrongs that have been done, the horrors that have been perpetrated, without pretence or exaggeration.

Similarly we can turn away from the world, throw up barricades, try to keep out anything that smacks of violence. Or we can look now with new eyes at films of Bosnia and Rwanda, at families standing in rubble mourning their dead in the latest war zone. We can feel new sympathy, do more, because it is now apparent that we are not exempt, we are like them in more ways than we believed.

We live in a place of extraordinary beauty. The beaches, the rock formations, the forests are still there in the autumn sunlight as they were last Sunday, as they will be—one hopes and trusts—for generations to come. When we look at them if we can remember these thirty-five deaths in a way that makes us live more humanely, more intensely, with broader sympathy, then some good may be brought out of this evil. The victims will not have died in vain and we will raise for them a memorial more fitting than anything wrought in stone.

NOTES

THE SITE

Bryant on violence: Interview with Martin Bryant, Professor Paul B. Mullin, *Mercury* (Hobart), 25 November 1996.

Journalist Lindsay Simpson: Lindsay Simpson, 'Port Arthur: The Future?' *Island*, 67, p. 94.

Peter MacFie, who: Peter MacFie, Port Arthur pamphlet and map for visitors to the Historic Site, undated.

Over the years: Ian Brand, *Port Arthur 1830–1877* (Tasmania: Jason Publications, 1975), p. 5.

Ministers of religion: Reverend John Manton, *The Isle of the Dead; or, The Burial Place at Port Arthur, Van Diemen's Land* (London: c.1845), p. 4.

George Greatbatch: Noel Greatbatch, 'The Greatbatch Family', in *Tasman Peninsula Chronicle*, no. 3, December 1987, pp. 30–2.

Other records create: Brand, p. 15.

In these conditions: *The Coal Mines Historic Site* (Parks and Wildlife Service: undated).

Frederick Mackie: Brand, p. 66.

Out in the bay: Manton, p. 4.

According to the: Richard Lord, *The Isle of the Dead, Port Arthur* (Hobart: 1976; 1995), p. 2.

Collins had been: Manton, p. 6.

Writing in his journal: John Mitchel, *The Gardens of Hell*, ed. Peter O'Shaugnessy (Sydney, 1988), p. 29.

The flogging yard: Robert Hughes, *The Fatal Shore* (London: 1987), p. 404.

The story of: Anthony Trollope, *Australia and New Zealand* (London: 1873).

Persons of all grades: *Mercury*, 27 December 1889.

More common than: Quoted in Peter MacFie, 'Letters from Lufra' (c. 1900), in *Tasman Peninsula Chronicle*, no. 4, November 1988, p. 35.

They would be: Letters of Percy Shearn, 1889 (Queen Victoria Museum and Art Gallery, Launceston).

Stories of the: Diary of E. W. Barwick quoted in Kath Noye, 'School Days at the Port', *Tasman Peninsula Chronicles*, no. 6, September 1991.

THE DAY

At 1.30 p.m.: Hughes, p. 399.

Later Mick Sargent: *Mercury*, 26 November 1996 (misdated 31 December).

As the men: *Mercury*, 1 May 1996.

But as the: The Queen v Martin Bryant in the Criminal Sittings of the Supreme Court held at Court number 7, Salamanca Place, Hobart, before His Honour the Chief Justice on Tuesday, the 19th day of November 1996, Transcript, p. 92.

Once Nicole and: *Mercury*, 30 April 1996.

As Damian Bugg: Transcript, p. 118.

Bryant gave a: Interview with Bryant conducted by Detective Inspectors Warren and Paine, played at Sentencing Hearing, Transcript, p. 232.

He just blocked: *Mercury*, 30 April 1996.

Once Pat Allen: *Mercury*, 26 November 1996 (misdated 31 December).

As night fell: John Hamilton, 'A Shattered Community Prepares to Reopen its Door to the World', *Weekend Australian*, 4–5 May 1996.

Tasmania's health team: *Mercury*, 26 November 1996 (misdated 31 December).

Later John Hamilton: *Weekend Australian*, 4–5 May 1996.

At the sentencing: Transcript, p. 142.

FALLOUT

No matter how: *Mercury*, 30 April 1996.

Damian Bugg: Transcript, p. 300.

The grief and: Transcript, p. 299.

David Capper: *Weekend Australian*, 26–27 October 1996.

The anxiety that: Elaine Reeves, 'No Time Limit: Personal Responses to Disaster', *Open Mind: Journal of the Tasmanian Association for Mental Health*, no. 15, Spring 1996, p. 6.

And there are: William De Maria in Damien Murphy, 'Society's Child', *Open Mind*, no. 15, Spring 1996.

As Damian Bugg: Transcript, p. 301.

Seven months after: *Saturday Mercury*, 23 November 1996.

Colin Prout: *Weekend Australian*, 26–27 October 1996.

Ben Bannister: Rosetta High School Parent News, Issue 4, 16 May 1996.

Mary Blackwood: Elaine Reeves, 'Backlash,' *Open Mind*, no. 15, p. 10.

Elaine Reeves: 'Backlash', p. 9.

Towards the close: Transcript, p. 307.

Andrew O'Brien: *Mercury*, 1 May 1996.

Justice Pierre Slicer: *Mercury*, 25 November 1996.

Ann Hillman: *Port Arthur Update*, no. 4, 3 October 1996 (Hobart: Dept of Community and Health Services).

The Premier: *Mercury*, 27 November 1996.

For the time: Michael Langley, 'The Historic Site Staff', *Port*

Arthur Update, no. 3, 2 September 1996.

All this led: *Mercury*, 17 January 1997.

This, too, was: Port Arthur Historic Site, Strategic Management Plan, Part 1: Executive Summary, p. 6.

And the prediction: *Sunday Tasmanian*, 22 December 1996.

RECOVERY

The committee set: *Gazette Newsletter*, 13 May 1996.

The Rosny Children's choir: *Gazette Newsletter*, 13 May 1996.

Still later there: *Port Arthur Update*, August 1996.

As the editor: *Weekend Australian*, 11–12 May 1996.

In his paper: Peter Grabosky, *Trends and Issues No. 33: Victim Impact Statements* (Australian Institute of Criminology), in Damian Bugg QC, 'The Implications for the Administrating of Justice of the Victims Impact Statement Movement', *Journal of Judicial Administration*, no. 5, 1996.

Mervyn and Mary Howard: Mary Thomas, 'Royal Hobart Hospital, 28 April 1996'.

At Port Arthur: *Mercury*, 26 November 1996 (misdated 31 December).

The Mercury, now: *Mercury*, 17 January 1997.

A Media Office: *Sunday Tasmanian*, 23 February 1997.

In memoriam
Port Arthur, 28 April 1996

Winifred Aplin

Wally Bennett

Nicole Burgess

Chung Soo Leng

Elva Gaylard

Zoe Hall

Elizabeth Howard

Mary Howard

Mervyn Howard

Ron Jary

Tony Kistan

Dennis Lever

Sarah Loughton

David Martin

Sally Martin

Pauline Masters

Alannah Mikac

Madeline Mikac

Nanette Mikac

Andrew Mills

Peter Nash

Gwen Neander

Ng Moh Yee

Antony Nightingale

Mary Nixon

Glenn Pears

Jim Pollard

Janette Quin

Helene Salzmann

Robert Salzmann

Kate Scott

Kevin Sharp

Ray Sharp

Royce Thompson

Jason Winter